Prayer from
Beginning to End

By the same author:

Learning about Private Prayer

Union with God:
The Teaching of St. John of the Cross

Prayer from Beginning to End

DESMOND TILLYER

*Vicar of St Peter's, Eaton Square, London
Area Dean, Westminster (St Margaret's) Deanery*

MOWBRAY
LONDON & OXFORD

First published 1987
by A. R. Mowbray & Co. Ltd,
Saint Thomas House, Becket Street,
Oxford, OX1 1SJ.

Typeset by Dentset, 35 St Clement's, Oxford OX4 1AB.
Printed in Great Britain by Biddles Ltd., Guildford

British Library Cataloguing in Publication Data

Tillyer, Desmond B.
Prayer from beginning to end.
1. Prayer
I. Title
248.3′2   BV210.2

ISBN 0–264–67037–X

For
My Mother and Father

CONTENTS

INTRODUCTION

To write a small book about the life of prayer from its initial, hesitant beginnings to its fulfilment in the vision of God is a task that is necessarily presumptuous, and beyond any hope of being wholly successful. I have been encouraged to do so, not because of my own confidence in completing the task, but through the generous promptings of friends and the willingness of Mowbrays to publish my efforts.

Also, I believe that such a book may make a small contribution towards meeting a need in the Church that comes from a dearth of experienced direction. The requirement of personal direction is indispensible for the health and safe progress of the soul, and yet many are forced to find their way to God without that necessary benefit. Perhaps this book will encourage those who are in that state to persevere and to continue to seek out a wise physician of the soul, as well as presenting the need for the training of more spiritual directors to those in authority who should be giving more time and attention to this central concern of the 'cure of souls'.

I have tried to follow the general principles of spiritual growth, set out by that great doctor of the spiritual life, St John of the Cross, although I have not quoted him directly. Rather, I have sought to express the essence of his teaching in terms which are more directly related to the present needs and understanding of Christians today. There is no attempt on my part to be autobiographical, because I suspect that while such an approach to writing about prayer can help some, yet its particularity will limit its value to others. However, there are inevitably 'nuggets' of myself hidden in the text which those who know me well will recognize. My hope is that they will not reduce the more general usefulness of the book.

A cardinal rule for reading books on the spiritual life is that they should be read prayerfully, seeking the guidance of the Holy Spirit. Therefore, if this book, or any section of this book, is not found to be useful or helpful, then put it on one side and seek guidance elsewhere. The Holy Spirit is telling you that it is not needful to you at this moment in your pilgrimage of faith, but perhaps something else may be. If, however, what is written does strike a chord in your experience, then ask the Spirit to reveal to you how to put into practice what he has shown you. If this book is helpful in leading the reader to make a practical commitment to seek God in prayer under the guidance of the Holy Spirit, then it will have achieved its purpose.

Finally, I must express my personal thanks to Ann Graham, who has patiently and skilfully typed the drafts and helped with the proof-reading. Without her expertise, the production of this book would have been so much more difficult, and I am grateful to her for all the hours she has put in to make the task easier.

Desmond B. Tillyer
Solemnity of Mary, Mother of God, 1986

ONE

Prayer at the Heart

To pray is to be human and to be human is to pray. Wherever we look for evidence of the existence and activity of human beings, we find ourselves looking at a religious animal. No matter how far back into prehistory we search, no matter where it is in the world, if remains of human life are found, so too are signs of prayer and ritual. Very rarely is a human body discovered without signs that it has been carefully laid out in death in accordance with religious rites; the earliest family hearth and home is a place of ritual and religious custom; the art of mankind from the first is religious by nature and intention. Altars, shrines, holy places abound wherever mankind leaves his mark. The evolution of the human race has been as much the emerging of man as a religious animal as any of his other characteristics recognized by anthropologists.

From the first, it is apparent that our ancestors grasped the significance and purpose of their lives through ritual, religious symbols and prayer, and used these as a means through which supernatural power was either placated or harnessed for the good of the individual and his community.

This extraordinary phenomenon, practised so universally by human beings, is not reflected, so far as we know, in any other part of creation. What is certain is that there is no evidence at present of prayer being practised by other forms of life on earth. Higher primates may make tools; many animals care for their young; family groupings are common at all levels of animal life; and some even domesticate and train other creatures to serve them. But none shows any evidence of spirituality. And so, the intriguing question is why prayer appears in the history of evolution as a recognizably conscious and chosen activity with the arrival of man.

Surely, it is more than just a coincidence that the evolution of prayer as a creaturely activity goes hand in hand with the evolution of the human mind as capable of self-awareness.

Man wakes up, as it were, to find himself conscious that he is alone in the world. He is surrounded by a hostile environment and must take stock of the dangerous, even precarious, position in which he finds himself. Around him, nature is 'red in tooth and claw' and his limited powers are stretched for survival. Until man developed his self-awareness, his predecessors in the evolutionary chain, like the rest of creation, had been governed by the blind forces of nature, by that unbending regime of instinct and received unconscious knowledge that governs with an iron rod every reflex reaction, every aspect of living and dying, without variation or purpose, except the survival of the fittest.

But now, newly emerged as recognizably human, with this remarkable ability to be aware of himself and his actions, mankind is no longer secure within the tyranny of immediate patterned response. He is faced with a new danger, a novel threat to his survival, beyond the brute powers of the natural order around him — he is faced with the possibility of choice, of freedom of action, and with the consequences of choice, namely, success or failure. Self-awareness gives us power over our lives, but it also brings in its wake the responsibility to choose well.

Furthermore, it makes us aware of other human beings in a way that no other creature is aware of its own kind. Here is another for whom life also has its successes and failures, and who is aware like us of the experience of estrangement from the rest of creation. Consciously recognized relationships are now open to man; real community, based on choosing to belong, becomes possible; the concept of the person as a recognizable individual is beginning to emerge. Man evolves as a creature for whom life takes on meaning, and his actions become significant to others as well as to himself. Being alive becomes, for the first time in creation, a matter of moral and spiritual concern.

Prayer appears at this point in creation as a necessity of life, because the human race discovers, apparently immediately, that the burden of this self-awareness, and all that follows from it, demands a helping hand if it is to be carried within the human heart, and that the helping hand we seek must come from outside our own limited resources and from outside the rest of creation. Other creatures pay no heed to our new needs. They treat us the same as before. Those new needs themselves are too many for us to bear unaided. Therefore, we look for a power beyond ourselves to give us the moral and spiritual strength we need to be human. The evolution of mankind brings into the progress of creation a new expressed need — the need for experienced supernatural good will — and prayer upon the lips of mankind is found to be the new way of meeting that need.

And what is true for our ancestors is true for us. This necessity of prayer is expressed in countless small ways every day. It happens when a hard-pressed business-man, leaving for the office to face a crucial management meeting, says to his wife, 'Wish me luck'; when we respond 'Bless you' to a sneeze; and when 'God, help me' springs to our lips at moments of danger or pain. Even the unbeliever is not adverse to seeking such supernatural assistance, almost without thinking or realizing what he is doing.

But, just because prayer is a phenomenon of human

experience throughout the ages, this does not make it necessarily what it claims to be, namely, the relating of a self-aware being with a source of power and influence outside himself. As a phenomenon, prayer could equally well be interpreted as the way mankind produces an echo of its own consciousness to alleviate its loneliness in an indifferent universe. The question is whether prayer evokes a response from outside ourselves or simply mirrors our own hopes and fears. Is the response to prayer referred to throughout human experience a reply from beyond ourselves or a reflection from within ourselves? Is necessity the mother of invention in matters of prayer, as she is claimed to be in so many other critical areas of life?

We have travelled as far in the study of prayer as the evidence of human history can take us, and there is no further mileage in it. The question of interpretation of that evidence now requires each person to make an assessment for himself on the basis of both his own experience and the experience of others. Wē have reached the point of faith. Either prayer provides mankind with the necessary and invaluable means of helping the human race to live in its environment from within its own resources, or prayer expresses mankind's need for a beneficial relationship with something greater than ourselves, beyond our own resources, which we believe will help us to live as human beings.

This faith estimate of the purpose of prayer is what divides the believer from the unbeliever. If we accept the estimate of the unbeliever, then religion is but a subsection of anthropology. But if not, then we have a whole new realm, that of faith and prayer, to consider. We are called to choose one way or the other in order to proceed any further. For the unbeliever, prayer is natural, primarily self-regarding, and geared to the struggle for survival. For the believer, prayer develops as a supernatural activity, focusing not on the self but on the divine, and shaped by the desire for relationship with that divinity.

This book is written for those who have made that act of faith, who have recognized for themselves, and discovered in the lives of holy men and women in this and other ages, that the only interpretation of the results of prayer that makes sense comes from the conviction that we find in prayer resources which are greater than our own powers, results which are not comparable with our own efforts, and benefits which are beyond our highest imaginings.

However, because of the essential link between self-awareness and prayer, we must beware of the simplification which distinguishes too sharply between 'beyond' and 'within'. To speak of prayer as a reaching out to the divine beyond ourselves is not to deny the description of prayer as equally travelling inwards to discover the divine within ourselves. To communicate with us, the divine has to touch us through our human nature. Otherwise, how is there to be relationship? Therefore, religious experience tends to hold together what is called the immanence and the transcendence of God, not as mutually contradictory ideas, but as necessary to any adequate description of divine nature as it touches our lives.

We are now moving beyond necessity into the realm of chosen action. Prayer as a human reflex-reaction to danger is a primitive condition to which we all revert from time to time, but it cannot sustain a developed relationship with the divine because it is not motivated to do so. The gods may have to be placated occasionally or perhaps they will withdraw their favours, but man has no natural interest beyond that fear to develop his life of prayer further than immediate requests for help. For to do more would imply that selfishness — or at least self-regard — is not the most effective driving force for human happiness or the highest interpretation of human interest and desire.

Once we discover this truth for ourselves — and we do so usually through a process of moral failure leading to a need for forgiveness — then we begin to move away from the concept of prayer as asking for instant supernatural help to overcome immediate personal dangers, towards a view of praying which recognizes the value of relationship with the divine, and the proper respect that the divine rightly requires from the human heart.

Such a development can be seen clearly in the rise of the Hebrew prophets in the eighth century BC with their assertion that true worship must go hand in hand with moral integrity. To engage in prayer without reformation of character is, in the prophetic understanding, to incur the condemnation of God. But such a view of prayer does imply certain things about the nature of the divine which need our consideration.

Up till this moment, we have not assumed anything particular about the nature of the divine, over and above the experience of divinity as other than ourselves and powerfully invasive of our lives. To draw further detail upon the face of the divine is to explore both what we call revelation and what we understand as faith. What is other than us is being brought into focus for us, partly through our own efforts and experience as a race and, more importantly, through the desire of divinity for self-disclosure.

But to affirm this much is to have moved a long way from our first tentative steps in coping with the impact of the divine upon us. The implications are that the divine both wishes to make known to us more of itself than we can work out for ourselves, and is capable of doing so.

To be specific, the Hebrew conviction is that the divine reveals itself, not as itself but as himself, and that the language of the person can be applied accurately to divinity. The idea of the divine gives way to language about God as personal. Also, God's otherness becomes seen as moral holiness. He wields more than just arbitrary power; rather, his actions are controlled by a personal will which is governed by his moral nature.

Such a step produces a profound revolution in religious understanding. It changes our approach to the divine from that of placating and supplicating an unknown, arbitrary, and possibly dangerous deity, into a systematic movement of heart and mind towards a God who welcomes and rewards those who wish to draw near to him. With this understanding of the holiness of God we have the reassurance we need, that he is consistent and upright in his ways with us and that we can rely on him to treat us in a predictable fashion. Gone are the fears of unjust retribution or fickle favouritism, in favour of a dependable relationship that we can trust. But, conversely, when we fail to live out God's moral law, then we find that we are in a worse state than we were before, because, when the divine was perceived as arbitrary and unknown to us, then our moral state was not integral to our approach. So the gain is the revelation of God's consistency towards us when we reach out to him, and the loss is the condemnation we discover within ourselves because we inevitably show inconsistency towards the God to whom we wish to draw near. The development that promises so much now reveals itself as a pit into which we fall, under the weight of the moral nature of God himself.

Prayer has opened up as a channel for communication between God and ourselves, and the message has been both hopeful and damning. The hope lies in the personal nature of God and that, therefore, he is able to understand us as personal. Indeed, the Hebrew description of the human race as 'made in the image of God' suggests that it is the personal in God which God has stamped upon our nature, in order to give us god-like qualities.

The damnation lies in the difference between what God asks of us as human beings, made in his image, and what in fact we prefer to do. The latter can only contrast badly with the former, even to the point of making us feel helpless and imprisoned by moral failure, unable to see any more what point there is in trying to relate to God, who makes moral demands upon us. Such is the debilitating effect of this universal human experience that guilt before God is woven into the very fabric of our consciousness. It is aptly described in the Bible in terms of a fall. The divine becomes once more oppressive, and the personal in divinity which seems to offer so much becomes identified with judgement.

The Jewish experience that followed the impact of the prophets upon the national consciousness is one of increasing domination by a sense of moral failure — what is called sin — and by a deepening sense of alienation from the God whom they both longed for and yet felt had moved beyond their unworthiness. Increasing emphasis on his otherness led to a tragic void at the heart of their religion, in which the personal relationship with God was principally expressed through an inhibitingly legalistic attitude to the keeping of the Jewish law, in the hope that something would turn up to rescue them from their dilemma.

Yet within this despair lay the correct intuition that the initiative lies with God, and that a moral God cannot ask so much of us and yet not give us the help we need to live worthily of him. And, if our failure has plunged us into a pit of sin, then surely that help from God will first lift us up out of that pit, and then set our feet on the mountain path to the summit of holiness. Both rescue and inspiration are needed.

Once again, it is the personal in God that comes to the fore. The need to take the initiative leads God to move beyond the teaching of moral principles through the prophets to the sending of his Son to rescue mankind from the pit of sin and to give us the means of living for God. The Christian doctrine of the incarnation of God as Jesus of Nazareth proclaims an even more fundamental assertion of the personal nature of God than the prophetic insight eight centuries earlier. It is a statement of faith that God is able to unite himself with our human nature in one person who retains both his full humanity and his full divinity, thus bridging the personal gap between God and man, and at the same time bringing about a reconciliation between God and man which rescues us from our failure and guilt through the forgiveness of sins, and gives us a secure basis upon which we can rebuild our lives for God. This reconciliation, rescue and renewal is achieved through the birth, death and resurrection of Jesus of Nazareth, and from that achievement flows the experience of prayer which approaches God 'through Jesus Christ our Lord'.

The channel of communication has become, in Jesus Christ, a discovery of personal sharing between the human and the divine that offers us a way of holding together our need for God, his moral nature, and our failure to be worthy of him. The personal in God is seen as forgiving and sustaining, so that his otherness becomes our goal, not our doom. We discover that to seek the presence of God is to find ourselves accepted and loved just as we are, and that prayer gives us an incentive to repent and seek reformation of character, without fear of condemnation and rejection by divine displeasure. God is not mocked, but no longer is he experienced as mocking.

This confidence of access to God through Jesus Christ is central to the Christian understanding of prayer. For the Christian, to pray is to express faith in God to God with both reverence for his holiness and the trusting simplicity of a child reaching out to a loving father. Indeed, trust in the fatherhood of God, revealed by Jesus as the heart of his relationship with God, is taught by

Jesus in his own prayer as the pattern for our praying. In his prayer, there is his own distinct combination of emphasis upon the holiness, the otherness, the will and the kingdom of God, coupled with straightforward petitions for our daily needs, for forgiveness and for protection, which come from a child-like trust in God's fatherly benevolence.

Seen in this light, the impact upon the apostles and the first disciples of praying with Jesus remains for us, on this side of his resurrection, in the experience of praying in Jesus and through Jesus. In fact, such praying as the first followers practised with Jesus before his death is intensified and interiorized for us who live in the presence of the risen Christ. The shift has been made from walking with Jesus to Jesus living and glorified in us, what St Paul calls praying 'in Christ'.

This praying 'in Christ' rests in turn upon the sacramental foundation of being 'in Christ', that is, upon Baptism and the union with the crucified and risen Lord which the sacrament effects. Our confidence lies in the joining of ourselves to Christ through the gift from God of being born again and grafted into his glorified body at the font. This grasp of the meaning of Baptism, set out by the writers of the New Testament, gives the person initiated both status as a child of God and confidence that Jesus has reconciled him to his heavenly Father.

The completion of the act of initiation through the gift of the Holy Spirit, followed by regular receiving of Holy Communion as a further sharing in the life of Christ, gives the Christian the very basis for believing and discovering that his prayer is heard before the throne of God. And from that prayer, rooted and grounded in Christ, there flow all the blessings which God wishes to shower upon us.

Prayer, as a channel of communication, opens up in Christ to become a means of receiving beneficially the influence of God upon the reformation of character which our awareness of his moral holiness requires of us. No longer is it a matter of fleeing in fear from the glory revealed. No longer does the Old Testament conviction that man cannot see God and live hold sway over our instincts. Rather, our instincts are now that we must draw near to God in order to benefit from his love for us, and that we can draw near with confidence because of the achievement of Jesus in reconciling us to him. There is now an element of attraction within the relationship between God and man, which comes from praying 'in Christ', and yet that attraction has none of the overtones of deadliness which we find in the attraction of a moth to a flame. Quite the contrary, it is an attraction which is designed to build up and perfect our humanity in and through our sharing in the divine humanity of Jesus.

Our prayer is becoming an engine of change. The primitive asking which is integral to our human nature is being placed in the context of changing our human nature so that our asking becomes less what we want and more what God wills. We are seeking to conform both our asking and our lives to the pattern of Christ, the perfect man who prayed, 'Not my will but thine be done'.

But in order to change we must desire to be changed; to wish to become perfect we are required to seek perfection from its source, namely, the nature of God. We need the grace of God to help us to change into the likeness of Christ, and that grace requires an openhearted and willing co-operation on our part. Grace perfects human nature through the steady application of human effort, sustained by the grace of God. And prayer is the activity of our race through which that grace flows into our lives daily and that steady effort is sustained. The channel of communication becomes a source of grace, refreshing and reviving our desire to grow into the image of Christ, and therefore becomes the fountain of all human virtue.

When such virtue is sought, and put into practice, its effect is none other than progressive amendment of life and reformation of character into the image of Christ. The person who is praying 'in Christ' is seeking Christlikeness, and in so doing, is being brought by the grace of God into human perfection, into what St Paul describes as mature manhood, the measure of the stature of the fullness of Christ.

To try to pray 'in Christ', without recognizing that this change is required, is to pray in vain, or at least in immaturity. Such praying rarely persists, but is likely to relapse into sub-Christian models.

However, for those who do recognize what God is asking of them, there is a goal which lies beyond the seeking of Christlikeness, indeed, a goal for which Christlikeness is preparing them. This goal is union with God. The divinity which our ancestors worshipped in ignorance and fear, placating and beseeching out of terror for their lives, has revealed himself as a God whose very nature is love and whose purpose in creation is to share his life with us in Christ. He has made us desiring creatures and planted such desires within us as can only be satisfied by finding their fulfilment in him. In the end, we are not drawn to virtue for its own sake — moralism is not synonymous with Christian faith — no, we are drawn to virtue because it makes us like Christ, so that we can find ourselves complete and entire as human beings in a union with God in which his nature is reflected in us and our nature is perfected in him.

True humanism requires the vision of God as its focus and union with God as its end, and prayer keeps that vision in focus and that union in view. Precisely of what that union will consist we must consider in more detail later, but suffice to say from the start that the Christian hope is for a union of persons which maintains our recognizable identity, not absorption; which sustains our individuality without the self-regard of individualism; which crowns our desiring with satisfaction, our striving with rest, our hope with possession, our faith with sight, our love with love, and transfigures the glory of man with the glory of God. Our goal is the fruition of the sacramental union we enjoy now in a union with God in heaven that brings us eternal joy in his presence.

TWO

The Changed Life

At the end of the last chapter we were being drawn to the perfection of prayer. Now we must turn back from its ultimate goal to its early beginnings.

Everyone prays naturally, but such prayer has little or no impact upon our awareness of God's call to a life of faith. To develop specifically Christian prayer, we need to be more than awake to our humanness. We need to be woken up to our human condition before God and to God's demand upon us. We need to come to faith.

How does such an awakening occur? Some will say that there is only one way, the 'born again Christian' way of violent change from gross unbelief into total conviction. But it is a heroic stance that reflects more the psychological needs of the convert and the converter than it does the requirements of God.

The method of change is often confused with the change itself, effected by the grace of God. Surely, it is the change which God achieves in us which is the more important, indeed, the basic matter in hand. How that change is achieved must be secondary and is likely to vary from person to person and from one set of circumstances to another. Since God's grace is given to us to perfect our human nature, change in that nature achieved under the influence, even impact, of that grace will not violate or destroy, but reorder and rebuild our humanity. The image of God within us, marred and distorted as it may be, remains the raw material upon which God works, changing us by degrees into the image of Christ. The divine work is one of transfiguration, not removal of one nature and replacement by another. The saints of God are rough hewn men and women like the rest of us, sculpted and polished by God's grace into the perfection of Christ, and the material upon which God labours to achieve his finished work is our given humanity, whose faults are to be turned into strengths and whose vices are to be reordered into virtues.

With such an understanding of God's purpose for us, we are wise to look for a variety of religious experience, a wide spectrum of response to the multi-coloured grace of God. All such experience is, of course, human, and therefore capable of being shared — there is enough in common for each of us to enter into and to understand the experience of others — but to seek to share requires that we do not seek to conform. God's grace is sovereign, but adaptable to each person's needs. Who are we to challenge that sovereignty by attempting to squeeze others into the personal mould of our individual experience? If we deprecate plaster saints, then we should not even begin to look for identikit sinners.

St Paul's moment of conversion on the road is one of sudden, total and absolute change. The zealous persecutor of the Church, virulent in his unbelief, consenting to the death of Stephen and determined to arrest Christians even in Damascus, is changed in a blinding moment of revelation. His secret pangs of conscience are laid bare by the grace of God and he comes suddenly to faith in the risen Christ. There is no more dramatic conversion in Christian literature, nor one so important, humanly speaking, to the history of the Church. But the great convert's letters offer scant evidence that he necessarily asked of others what he himself went through. Indeed, with other experience already in the Church, how could he? The difference between him and St Peter could not, in this respect, be greater.

St Peter, in contrast, vacillated to and fro between

impetuous belief — 'You are the Christ, the Son of the living God' — at Caesarea Philippi, and cowardly denial — 'I do not know the man' — in the courtyard of the High Priest's palace. If we are to believe the legend of 'Quo vadis, Domine?', then such vacillation was in his character till the end. This is a man, converted not from gross unbelief to total conviction, but a man converted from nominal faith to painful discipleship. Not for St Peter convincing trust all the time, but a following of Christ, marked with failure of nerve, bitter repentance and amendment of life. For some, faith means living with doubt, trust is discovered through failure or denial, and conviction holds us fast though it often wavers under test.

Most of us live, by grace, between the experience of St Peter and St Paul, with sometimes the ennui, the gloom of doubting Thomas thrown in for good measure, and are called by God to do so as the way of the cross works out for each one of us as the way to perfection and to union. To imagine that it ought to be otherwise for ourselves — or worse, that it is otherwise for others, and especially for Church leaders — is to do ourselves a great disservice and to seek what is impossible, namely, a different human nature from the one that God has given us. We are not to look for some divine act of replacement which slots into our life a new spare part from a heavenly stock of already perfected humanities, waiting to be supplied to new converts. Rather we are to trust that God is working his purpose out in us as we are — we are not yet as he would have us be, but that will emerge under his influence out of the raw material that we are now.

To some, such a grasp of the life of faith could be understood as a licence for laxity, or at least, passivity. If God is willing to perfect my humanity by his grace, why should I bother myself with what Christ calls the way of the cross? Is not the temptation to let such a way become not a following of Christ but a following of self, or at least, a resting in the self that I know and find so comfortable? Yes, it is, if you are the sort of person who is comfortable as he is or tempted to believe that there is no improvement of self worth striving for or perfection remotely likely to be achieved. But this is not Christ's way. To be accepted as we are is but the first step in a series of steps towards God. To believe that because God accepts us as we are he is satisfied with what we are is quite false — his acceptance is designed to give us confidence, not in ourselves as worthy of him, but in him as wanting us for himself. He accepts us as we are to encourage us to move towards him in holiness. He calls us to change as the means of growing to perfection; he calls us to respond as the method of finding our true selves; he calls us to follow, as the way of becoming like our master. We have here, not a licence for laxity or passivity, but a charter for progress, as God's grace transforms our responsive humanity from one degree of glory to another into the measure of the stature of the fullness of Christ, that mature manhood which has been created, redeemed and inspired for its goal, union with God.

Any desire to rest and remain at less than this vision and to find peace and contentment in anything less than this union is to deny the grace of conversion and to seek to return to unbelief. Forms of conversion do differ from person to person, and the forms themselves are only relevant in that they are the means used by God to achieve a grace-faith relationship between himself and us, that will enable us to give ourselves to the Christian life, starting where we are and being built up into sanctity. What is important is the sort of change which God is looking for in us and seeks to bring about in us, through the grace of conversion and with our co-operation.

This change has already been described as being

woken up to the reality that knowing we are human is not enough. Put positively, it means becoming aware that we need God and God's blessing to live creatively as human beings. It implies facing the truth about ourselves, that we are flawed, faulty creatures, debasing and despising our very nature as well as God's creative grace within us by our treatment of ourselves and of others, and our failure to live as God would have us be.

Conversion is a change within us from one state into another state of existence. We are leaving behind a way of living as a human being without faith in God, and embarking on a way of living as a human being who believes and trusts in God. Let us examine this change more closely.

Pride is the natural condition of fallen man. This vice means that we have a built-in tendency to exaggerate our worth and to belittle our needs and our faults.

It is the sin of Adam and Eve in the myth of the fall that they presume too much, they take too much upon themselves and make an unrealistic bid for power which would make them like God, knowing good and evil. They fail because their presumption cannot be sustained. Their humanity is not able to bear the burden that their pride has placed upon it. So, they hide in the garden from the presence of God, knowing in themselves that they have become alienated from him. The ensuing story is one of alienation not only from God, but also between human beings. Cain kills Abel, and the pride of the first act of folly leads to increasing offences as man's inhumanity to man opens up a chasm between us, both to the mutual loss of every human being and his neighbour and to the mutual loss of God and the human race as a whole.

Pride is the destruction of harmony between God and creature, based on our true worth in his eyes, and his infinite worth to us. Our race replaces this harmony with a false and inflated ego-trip in its desire to be godlike, on its terms and by its own devising, together with a drive to remake our need for God into gods made in our own image, products of our own pride, to be manipulated and coerced into doing our will and satisfying our wishes. And so we make gods of the things we use to enhance our self-esteem and strengthen our security — money, reputation, possessions, sex, violence, ultimately making the self into the focus of our worth, our worship, our very purpose in life. No wonder pride is seen as the source of all sin, and sin is equated with unbelief! Thus far has the human race fallen away from the purposes of God, and the consequences are revealed to us every day in the newspapers, on the television screen — and in our own hearts, if we will listen to them. False beliefs, debased values, reduced vision, disorderly living, selfishness at the centre of our being feed off one another to make us fallen indeed.

We certainly pass on this pride to our children by teaching them from birth to value the disorderly and self-seeking characteristics that we ourselves possess and esteem. And who can tell how far these manifestations of human pride have influenced the genetic traits we hand on to our children? God alone knows the full extent of the damage we have inflicted on ourselves and our children. The drastic and costly remedy which God employs to restore us to our true selves, the incarnation, death and resurrection of his only Son, is his indication to us that the consequences of pride have been far more serious than we could ever imagine.

The antidote to pride is humility, that supernatural virtue which counteracts the effects of our proud foolishness. Humility is now the supernatural condition open to fallen man, come to faith in the true and living God. This virtue, offered to us by the grace of God and developed within us by our response of obedience to that grace, reverses the built-in tendency common to us all of exaggerating our worth and belittling our needs and faults.

If pride makes this mistake in true judgement, if pride gets wrong the realistic estimate of the place and worth of human nature in God's scheme of creation, then humility is the virtue that steadily brings round our consideration of ourselves into line with the worth that God places on us. What is this estimate? It is none other than this, that we are created in the image of God, redeemed sinners brought back into the fold of God's purposes through the grace and love of Jesus Christ, God's only Son, and made for union with God in eternal happiness. In short, our great worth lies not in our own proud estimate of ourselves but in God's infinite and undaunted will to bring us to perfection in Christ and to make us one with him. This is our true worth, our lasting security, our ultimate purpose for living, besides which the worth and esteem, which our pride seeks through the exploitation of people and things, crumbles into insignificance and the worship of self that pride requires dissolves into ridiculous futility. How tragic and yet comic our presumption is! How much havoc and destruction it has wrought and still wreaks upon God's world! What fools we have been to deceive ourselves in this way! We mock ourselves, exchanging our true worth for trinkets and baubles of no lasting value.

But, because the gift of humility is needed by us after we have tasted the bitter fruits of pride, the awareness that humility brings, once it begins to fill us with its virtue, reveals that pride has left a tainted legacy. For humility reveals not only that we are called to accept ourselves as we are, made for union with God in Christ, but also that we are not yet as God would have us be, not yet worthy of the vision and the union that is our goal, because of the effects of pride remaining within us. Humility contains elements of both what we are now and what we are not yet. The consequences of man's long love of pride continue to influence for the bad our choices, our faith, our commitment to God, and to undermine the purposes of God in us by checking our desire to co-operate fully with his grace.

Conversion from pride and unbelief to humility and faith is not a once and for all event which produces a necessary daily improvement for the rest of our lives. One step towards God is not enough to attain to him. Faith has to be worked out as daily faithfulness; humility has to be put into practice every day by means of daily obedience to the will of God, the acceptance of humiliation when pride is revealed in disobedience and denial, and when others reveal by their holiness that we have not walked as far as they along the way of the cross.

For humility is the mark of Christ's life that is the foundation of his sinless perfection. That humility is at root obedience to the Father's will in his acceptance of our human nature in the womb of the Virgin Mary, in his proclamation of the sovereignty of God by his teaching and his miracles, in his willingness to suffer for God's kingdom and to put himself entirely into the hands of God for the sake of that kingdom, in his acceptance of a life of sacrifice which reached its fulfilment on Calvary, and in his joy that the Father raised him from the dead so that he might be with us as our Saviour to the end of time. This humility, so pure, complete and perfect in Christ, is not tainted by the effects of pride within him, but is tested by the effects of pride in others as they reject him and seek to destroy him. This way of the cross will come to us also if we truly seek obedience to God and place his kingdom first in our lives. As our pride is driven out, and its effects within us are reduced, so we shall change into the likeness of Christ, and, in so doing, find that others will take offence at us and treat us, from the depths of their pride, as they treated Christ. In a fallen world, redeemed by Christ, those who follow him will be tested as he was, in proportion to the changes that humility has achieved in them to conform them to him.

The evidence for this truth can be seen in every age in places where the Church is persecuted and oppressed by unjust and tyrannical governments which cannot bear the witness of Christian men and women to their faith. It is experienced within families or at work where Christians find themselves held in contempt, mocked, ridiculed, rejected or ignored by those who cannot bear the change that faith brings about in the believer. And it is discovered in our own hearts, when we find we have mixed feelings about other Christians whose transparent holiness clearly indicates that they have progressed further than we in their pilgrimage of faith. Not for nothing has the theme of holy warfare resounded down the ages in Christian spirituality; but it is a strange fighting where pride is resisted with humility, oppression with love, affliction with patience, and where Christ crucified is our banner and our example.

What, then, are the signs of conversion? For the person like St Paul, who has a dramatic experience of grace which causes a decisive break with the past, the question may seem superfluous. But, for the person like St Peter, there may be a need to untangle some of the conflicting feelings in order to discover how the grace of God is at work within.

First, there is the gift of faith, a profound, transforming revelation of belief in God at the heart of our life and a deep, earnest desire to trust God with our life from now on. This gift of faith may come as it did to St Paul, in a flash of divine light, penetrating his whole being, or it may steal upon us gently and silently until one day we are aware, we know not how or why, that we really believe and we truly wish to trust God with our lives. We may look back and see God's hand carefully weaving a pattern in our life up to that moment, so that everything 'comes together' and we see that we have believed for some time without realizing it. This may happen to churchgoers with nominal commitment to God and to those who have had no apparent previous religious affiliation, to whom the moment comes as a surprise. For some, both types of experience are compelling and convince them for all time that they are called to live by faith. But for others, the moment may wear off — even if it was of the Pauline variety — and need to be recalled and reaffirmed regularly. Either we may do the recalling and reaffirming by committing ourselves to that past moment as true then and still true now, or God may recall and reaffirm that moment for us, giving us a new impulse of his grace to repeat or enhance or develop the original experience. Such rediscovering of God's converting power is not an adverse comment on previous moments of conversion, but simply the way God acts in us to meet the needs we have because of the type of personalities we are. No one way of coming to faith is superior to another — all are tested, not by their beginnings, but by their continuation in a life of faithfulness to God.

Secondly, there is the gift of repentance. Sorrow for sin and the rejection of evil are signs that conversion is real. Any deepening of relationship between God and ourselves, any move into faith cannot but lead us to reflect upon our unworthiness before God and the grace he has poured out upon us. Like St Paul, our conscience is laid bare and we see ourselves as sinners in earnest. Confession of our sins and discovery of his forgiveness are necessary if we are to stand before this God who calls us to faith and to holiness. For those who have not been baptized, like St Paul, this is the moment to go down into the waters of the font, confessing our sins and rising again forgiven, to a new life united with Christ. But for those who are already baptized, this moment of conversion is a moment for stirring up the regenerating grace of baptism within us, making it fruitful in our lives and setting us on the path that Christ in us has prepared for us. Repentance here can mean using the sacrament of Penance, perhaps for the first time, or finding absolution in the tears that start to flow as the grace of God gently but firmly pierces our hearts and releases the sorrow for sin welling up inside. When Jesus looked at St Peter in the courtyard, that look broke his heart, and it does the same to some of us when we come to faith.

Thirdly, conversion leads us naturally and appropriately to commitment to God, to his will, to prayer, to worship, to the sacraments. We find ourselves wanting to pray, to receive Holy Communion, to join ourselves with other Christians in worship, to seek the will of God and to give ourselves to that will in loving obedience. This usually leads to rapid and serious changes in our life — the way we live, what we live for, how we assess our values, priorities, purpose, meaning of life — and may lead to new vocations. Our life is being changed under the good hand of God and we are finding ourselves in a new way through his influence and guidance. Our feet are being set on a new path, and we feel led by God to rethink and reorder our future as a follower of Christ.

How does such a conversion come about? God uses many and various ways. He may act directly as with St Paul — a moment, dramatic or not as the case may be, when the person converted knows that God has done this thing in him. But much more often, God uses intermediaries as his agents to bring his grace to us — a particular act of worship, or while receiving Holy Communion or making one's confession, a moment in prayer, or silence or stillness, the reading of Scripture or some other book, an individual sent by God who touches our life with an apt word or gesture or by an act of love, through the pondering of creation and its beauty, in the midst of suffering, or pain or moral dilemma, through the influence of conscience when our sin afflicts us severely. In these and many other ways, God acts to convert us from pride and unbelief to faith and humility. In so doing, God gives us what we need to find ourselves convinced that he is calling us to serve him and that from now on our life will find its meaning in that service.

A serious decision for God has been made, compelling us to go on in faith and repentance to commit ourselves to him, and as an integral part of that serious decision, the practice of prayer will need to develop in order to carry the enhanced awareness of God that conversion has brought to us. But before this can really take wings, some further aspects of the converted life must be considered, those of dependency, goodness and enthusiasm. To these we now turn.

THREE

Mature Dependence

The title of this chapter may surprise, or even shock, the reader. It is intended to. We live in an age that admires independence and maturity, and associates the two. Apparently, a mature person 'stands on his own two feet' and is 'not beholden to anyone'. Such sentiments, indoctrinated into children by adults who sincerely believe these principles, are perpetuated almost without thinking about them. Both maturity and independence are seen as desirable and linked together as though they naturally belong together. Unfortunately — or, rather, fortunately — they do not.

For an age that promotes independence, there is surprisingly little analysis as to what the word means. It is used as a general term, denoting such widespread and unrelated concepts as financial independence and emotional independence. We may be encouraged to admire a man of independent frame of mind and to envy a woman of independent means. One may produce strikingly original thoughts, the other have freedom from poverty; on the other hand, neither result may follow.

However, behind all notions of independence, there lies the concept of freedom, and the purpose of independence is to present us with the opportunity to exercise certain freedoms, both freedom from particular constraints and freedom to pursue chosen courses of action. Financial independence should give us freedom from depending on others for money and freedom to spend our money as we wish. Political independence should give a nation freedom from undue influence upon its political decisions by other nations and freedom to make its own political choices unilaterally.

These last two examples begin to ring warning bells. How can we be entirely financially independent, since we depend upon others to help us create our wealth? How can any nation be totally unconcerned about the consequences of its political choices upon its neighbours? The truth is, independence is a much vaunted principle presented to us as ideal, but in practice only observed in the breach.

And what is true of the examples given is even more so in the case of emotional and personal independence. No matter how much we claim to stand on our own two feet, in fact we are all beholden to at least someone, if not to many people. It is a law of nature that we survive by interdependence. The solitary is doomed because he has no support to fall back on in adversity. Indeed, it is precisely those aggressively independent people in public who often require a reliable dependent relationship in private from which to draw support, recuperate and recover confidence for the fray. Is not this an integral part of the purpose of marriage, not only between parent and child but also between husband and wife? Is not this a large function within friendship and an essential ingredient of comradeship and *esprit de corps*?

And if this is so on a wide personal level, then we must admit that emotional independence hardly exists at all. Not only do our emotions need outlets and objects to which to attach themselves, but in doing so we become dependent on the outlet and the object. Moreover, such outlets and objects need not even be human. Animals provide countless people with emotional satisfaction, and become outlets for all sorts of human needs. It is no coincidence that elderly people with pets that depend upon them generally keep physically and mentally fitter than those who have no pets to care for. Is this not so, not only because the pet depends on its owner, but also because the owner has an emotional dependence upon the pet?

And we can take this matter further. Even inanimate objects become receptacles for emotional needs — favourite chairs provide rest and security; regular routines give the day meaning and order; many people fend off depression or frustration by spending money on new clothes or gadgets for the house; a sense of inadequacy or failure can be sunk in alcohol or drugs. The range of objects on which we human beings become dependent in order to meet our emotional needs is as extensive and as varied as the needs themselves, and we rarely have to look far before we find one to hand to use in this way.

And if independence is largely a figment of our imagination, probably to bolster our unstable pride, what of maturity? Here we are on very different ground. Maturity is to do with the development of our human potential, so that the gifts and qualities within us become realized in our lives. To believe in maturity is to believe in the possibility of human growth for all of mankind. Such maturity will take many forms, including physical maturity, intellectual development, emotional insight, self-control and stability, good personal relationships, ability to love and be loved, balanced moral principles, personal happiness and fulfilment, courage and integrity in the face of adversity and suffering, well developed spiritual insights and experience.

Of course, in a fallen, sinful environment, such a well-rounded maturity is as much an ideal as independence, but unlike the latter, maturity has at least the merit of being a quality worth striving for, even if its realization *in toto* is unattainable. However, the striving has in itself certain dangers. It can easily become selective and partial because this is easier than all-round development to maturity. Attention to our strengths may lead us to underestimate our weaknesses. For example, physical strength may be turned to harm, unless it is brought under the control of good moral principles; emotional strengths may be used destructively, unless held within a mature self-control that prevents emotional havoc being done to others; intellectual development may be used to outwit and humiliate those who are close to us, unless we have learnt the meaning of love. In these and many other ways, human beings are a mixed economy of the mature and the infantile, and aspects of both interact negatively and violently upon one another. Developed faculties despise the undeveloped ones, and the undeveloped faculties in turn smart under their humiliation and neglect, and surreptitiously undermine and thwart the developed ones. So it is that we find ourselves at war within ourselves, our pride tearing us apart internally as our various faculties refuse to harmonize for the common good.

And such internal strife is more easily borne if we redirect it beyond ourselves and make others the recipients of the strains and tensions, antagonisms and frustrations, that we experience within ourselves. The popular demand for maturity can so easily breed a hydra-headed monster in which others become the reason for our own failure to grow up as individuals, and society carries not only the blame, but also develops the destructive tendencies that are within ourselves. And once a particular trait becomes developed in society, it feeds back upon us so that the two aspects of the individual and the corporate become inextricably intermeshed, and we are faced with massive difficulties in making any attempt to remedy the situation. Leaders should be especially careful not to inflict nations and institutions with their own internal dissent, lest they leave upon them a mark of their leadership which mirrors their sin only too closely.

Is not this failure of maturity part of the tragic consequences of the fall, of that pride which strikes out for independence? Has not pride entered every faculty of our make-up, dividing us within, as different aspects of our one self struggle together? How often we meet people whose lives are distorted or maimed by this internal warfare — men and women of good intellectual development who are afraid of their feelings and disabled by them; people with a developed moral sense who are intellectually rigid and incapable of compassion; people of faith who are frightened of intellectual questions or even the physical aspects of their own body, and so on.

Yet, in God's eyes, we are created one person, physical, intellectual, emotional, moral, spiritual. These varied aspects of the one self are intended for harmony, so that we may flourish as human beings and find maturity as whole people. We are intended for mature manhood, for the measure of the stature of the fullness of Christ. He is humanity as God intends us to be. His perfect and sinless balance and stability are our inspiration and our goal as human beings called to be like him. And at the heart of that maturity lies a recognition and a living out of our interdependence within, between our human faculties, in which we give all of them their due worth and they respond by working creatively and co-operatively together. Indeed, there is no 'I' independent of these faculties; rather they together are the 'I' that exists now and the 'I' that emerges as they progress to maturity. It may be that one faculty, the intellect, comes to have a controlling or guiding influence over the rest, but that does not mean either that the other faculties feel down-trodden or that the intellect treats them badly and without due respect.

One of the striking qualities about Jesus is that his internal peace, his personal integration based on humility, his mature interdependence within, radiate outward from himself in such a way that a mutually beneficial bond is made between him and those around him. Others give themselves to him and come to depend on him and he gives himself to them and comes to depend on them. His relationship with Peter, James and John runs through the Gospels as an example of this accepted mutual dependence. The women who ministered to his needs had received first his ministrations towards them. He depended on his mother from his conception, and she stood by him on Calvary, and allowed him to look after her by giving her into the care of the beloved disciple. And above all and in all these dependent relationships was his dependence upon God. An integral part, indeed the very source, of his maturity, is revealed in his spiritual maturity, and that spiritual maturity is summed up in his prayer, 'Not my will, but thine be done'. He accepts that he is sent to do the Father's will, and surrenders his life to that end in obedience to his Father's command. His maturity is rooted in this willing, chosen acceptance that his life depends on his Father, and that its purpose and true fulfilment lies in loving obedience to him. In the temptations, he rejects any spurious independence and pride in order to sacrifice his life in the name of dependence and humility.

And this is our calling also, to sacrifice our lives in the name of dependence and humility as the way to full maturity. We need to acknowledge and to be happy to accept our dependence on others and their dependence on us, in different ways with many people — parents, brothers and sisters, spouses, children, friends, fellow-workers, the interlocking pattern of society, relying as it does upon our mutual sense of responsibility and integrity. We depend on others and they depend on us, and together we help one another to grow to maturity. Indeed, the healing power of good relationships with others helps us to be on good terms with ourselves, and this in turn enables us to build better relationships with others. Just as much is destructive and competitive in society and within ourselves, equally in both there is much that is constructive and co-operative, working for our common good.

And over and above, and at the same time, within and throughout this growth to maturity through dependence is the spiritual maturity that binds all together in a loving, obedient dependence upon God and his will, to bring our lives to their true purpose, oneness with God, in and through our commitment to others and our commitment to him. How different this is from the shallow and spurious vision of mankind as 'come of age', standing independent of God, mankind and nature, a demi-god with enormous powers and un-limited possibilities. Is not this vision more of hell than of heaven, a restatement of the Fall in a twentieth-century form? The rabbinic aphorism that 'Every man is the Adam of his own soul' has come upon us with a vengeance!

For true courage requires of us not that we make yet another bid for independence, not that we repeat the sin of Adam's transgression, but that we have the courage to accept and embrace the fact that we are dependent creatures, dependent on one another, dependent upon the world we live in, and first and foremost, dependent upon God, our creator and provider. To face this need within ourselves is the beginning of all growth to maturity, in which spiritual growth integrates, reforms and inspires all other aspects of our quest for maturity. Without this fundamental reversal of heart and mind, nothing can be achieved. But if we are converted to this vision of human happiness, then growth is possible.

Dependence upon God is a way of life, or rather, the way to life which is life indeed. Jesus shows us that it is so, and his maturity validates the way of discipleship as the way of the cross. His sacrificial life in the service of his Father points us to sacrifice as the cost of finding maturity through dependence in a fallen world. 'Not my will, but thine be done', is no easy recipe for living, and will bring us up against not only our own conflicting desires to do otherwise, but also up against the conflicting desires of others who do not hold the same vision that we have.

One aspect of this sacrifice is the giving of ourselves to prayer. If conversion spurs us to begin to pray, then our acknowledged dependence upon God requires us to consolidate that beginning into a practice of prayer that will last, and become integrated into the very rhythm of our lives. Furthermore, because that dependence upon God is, we believe, necessary for our maturity, our prayer becomes not only integral to our lives, but a point of growth within our lives so that growing maturity in prayer goes hand in hand with all other aspects of our development into the image of Christ. Indeed, prayer, as a channel of communication and grace between God and us, is more than a point of growth — it is the point from which spiritual growth comes and, therefore, in so far as we open the whole of ourselves to God, the point through which our integration into maturity takes shape under the guiding hand of God.

But what is this God like, that we should give ourselves to him so fully and completely? How does he reveal himself to us through the inspiration of the human mind and through his own self-disclosure in Jesus Christ?

First of all, any God to whom we give ourselves must have the oneness, wholeness, we are seeking for ourselves. Therefore, faith that God is one and at one with himself lies at the heart of commitment. This oneness is not primarily numerical, but implies a united, consistent, harmonious divine life which offers us the goal we are seeking. Thus, Jesus reveals that this divine oneness is for God the rich life of the Holy Trinity,

Father, Son and Holy Spirit, bound together in an eternal love flowing from one person to another in perfect giving and receiving and returning again. So it is that the loving obedience of Jesus, the incarnate Son, to the Father is part of the Son's eternal loving obedience to the Father in the Godhead. Jesus, God and man, sacrifices his life lovingly and willingly to the Father's will and so brings into time and the work of salvation, the sacrificial love that the Son has for the Father in all eternity. His sonship on earth is consistent with his sonship in heaven.

Secondly, the prophetic message that God is personal and loving is confirmed in the incarnation, and Jesus reveals that the personal nature of God invites us to seek a union with him that brings us to personal fulfilment in the vision of God, and not to loss of all selfhood in an abyss of impersonal deity. Furthermore, as we have seen, the love of God is shown in Jesus to be suffering love, love that seeks the lost and brings home the outcast, love that sacrifices itself to save others from their sin and reconcile them to God. Thus, this personal God who suffers for us and in us carries our suffering within his heart and makes our suffering a means of sharing in the work of Jesus through the way of the cross. Suffering ceases to be destructive, unless we wish it to be, and becomes, if we choose so, a means of growing into union with God. Suffering does not break down our maturity unless we respond with like, returning evil for evil. Instead, it tests our maturity and invites us to deepen our dependence upon God.

Thirdly, we look for a God who is infinite and eternal, so that all things and all times are within his understanding and his compassion. We are wary at the idea of sharing deep and vulnerable aspects of our life with people who will not give us adequate personal support to face the truths that we reveal in so doing. We require of them not only attention and understanding, but also time and availability. 'Ships that pass in the night' relate only superficially. We desire more, if relationship is to mean more than acquaintance. And what is true of other people is supremely true of God. We desire a God whose love, attention and support is permanent and all-embracing if we are to unburden our deepest, most painful and most vulnerable aspects of ourselves to him. Only an infinite, eternal God can give us what we desire, because only then can we be sure that he will not fail us or forsake us. It is this confidence of Jesus in his Father that enabled him to open his heart to him in the garden of Gethsemane and to accept the cross as integral and necessary to his obedience. Even his cry from the cross, 'My God, my God, why hast thou forsaken me?' is resolved in his faithful surrender at the last, 'Father, into thy hands I commend my spirit'. And it is this confidence of Jesus, proved to be well-grounded in experience, that enables us to follow his example and open our hearts to the infinite and eternal God whom Jesus taught us to address as Father.

Fourthly, we find ourselves faced endlessly with the changes and chances of time and place, and our lives have little lasting stability. New circumstances may bring fresh opportunities for growth to maturity, but if our one lasting dependent relationship is to be with God, then he must be independent of the sort of changes that we undergo. We rely upon him being unchanging, free from the need to adapt to circumstances, fully and permanently consistent within himself and towards us at all times and in all places, in order to be able to turn to him with confidence from within the altering circumstances of our lives. This reintroduces the idea of independence and freedom, and we see that what is an unattainable ideal for man is unattainable precisely because it is of the nature of God alone to be independent and free, and our attempts to gain both are part of our fallenness and our proud fantasy that we can be godlike. The way forward for us is to attach ourselves in dependent love to the God who never changes and in doing so find that we grow detached from the circumstances of our lives, because they do not measure up to the fulfilment we find in God and are not meant to do so.

Lastly, we seek a God who is responsive, who is not indifferent to us or aloof from our needs. We are desiring creatures, and we believe that God has made us so, with a purpose in mind. We desire happiness, we seek fulfilment, we look for satisfaction, we rejoice in moments of fullness and sorrow at deprivation and loss. We are not content with a view of life that teaches us to hope for little and to settle for what there is — we naturally want more.

Of course, sin has made this wanting disorderly and turned our desiring into wrong directions, making us seek inadequate and false means of meeting our desires. This misdirection of our desiring is called concupiscence, and it is the bane of every human being's life. We desire wrongly and we pay the penalty. When we achieve what we desire, it proves unable to meet our deepest needs and may even inflame our desires further along the downward path towards self-centredness and loss of God. We become a prey to our hopes and our fears, our joys and our griefs, hardly able to bear to live without some immediate gratification to hand.

But God does not wish this to be our end; rather our end is to be with him and to enjoy him for ever. This is the reason why he has created and redeemed us. Therefore, we look to God to provide us with the means to satisfy our desiring, to fulfil our wanting, to meet our need for happiness. We seek a God who responds to our condition by offering himself to us as our fulfilment. We desire him to be the one who will share with us his own full and lasting happiness. So it is that the Christian life is that of seeking and finding our heart's desire in union with God, so that we are content with what we have of created things, because we are in touch with a fulfilment that goes beyond what they can offer.

Jesus shows in his prayer that centring our life on God does not disappoint us if we persevere. For him, that union was immediate in his total obedience to God and his kingdom. He tells us to do what he has done, to seek first God's kingdom and his righteousness, and then all else will fall supernaturally into place through the grace of God in our lives. If we make attachment to God our first priority, as Jesus did, then we shall be satisfied and receive our true heart's desire, and know in this life a foretaste of the union which God offers to all who desire him. We may lose all else, or be powerfully tempted by sin to try to find happiness in created goods, but once we have glimpsed the vision that shall be and tasted the union to come, then we shall find that our disorderly desiring begins to lose its grip on us and our life will centre more and more upon God and his will.

Out of this growing relationship between ourselves and the God who is our goal and our purpose in life, we discover that the freedom which God enjoys begins to be imparted to us. That freedom is not licence to act as we wish, but freedom increasingly to do the will of God. We discover that he is the one 'in whose service is perfect freedom'. Of course, this freedom is not freedom from dependence upon God, but the fruit of growing like Christ.

Jesus treated every person he met as made in the image of God and therefore of infinite dignity and value in the eyes of God, irrespective of human reputation. He also knew that his own reputation was as nothing compared with the confidence the Father placed in him because of his loving obedience to his will. These two truths allowed Jesus to approach other people with a freedom and a boldness that shocked his contemporaries, amazed his followers, and delighted the outcasts of society. He brought to them healing, good news and peace; he reconciled them, through the forgiveness of sins, to God and to their true selves as children of God; he entrusted them with his work as partners in the proclamation of the kingdom. He gave them back what they thought they had lost for ever, their dignity in the eyes of God, and showed them that they had much to offer those other members of society who refused to hear the message of Christ.

As we grow more like him, so we shall find that we too become free to risk entering into relationships with others whom society finds 'untouchable'. Just as Jesus touched others, so too are we, and for the same reason, to bring healing, good news and peace, reconciliation to God through the forgiveness of sins and to their true selves as children of God. Like Christ, the attitudes of society mean less to us as the service of God means more. This is what St Augustine means when he says, 'Love God and do as you wish', because if we love God, then what we wish is to do what he wishes for us. Again, it is in the practice of prayer that we discover the significance of this new freedom to risk our lives for God, and what it means for us in each particular situation which he places before us.

We have now come back to true maturity, to that quality of life which is lived in loving dependence upon God, conformed to his will, surrendered to his purpose, dedicated to the following of Christ, fulfilled in obedience, and worked out in a new found freedom from things which releases us to be Christ to the world. That world needs us to speak his word of eternal life, and through prayer God urges us to do so in his name.

FOUR

The Primacy of Goodness

Until now, I have hardly touched on the question of goodness, not even as a quality of God's being. Now is the moment to remedy this omission. My reason for waiting until this point has been twofold. First, ideas of goodness and 'the good' are tossed around in everyday speech without much thought as to meaning. We regularly pray for 'the common good', though what that is remains mysterious, to say the least, to most of us. Secondly, God is described as good, as though it were natural to do this, whereas it is far from obvious that this is so. There are in some religions good and evil gods, and in some Old Testament books, the behaviour of God is certainly suspect of evil intent, while in others — Job and Ecclesiastes — God seems indifferent to good and evil, being beyond both in his inscrutability.

Plato's view of God is as 'the Good', which appears to be an impersonal principle of virtue, order and positive attributes, such as truth, beauty, justice, etc. But all this is a long way from the biblical understanding of goodness, and it is to this that we must turn for enlightenment if we are to grasp the meaning of goodness in the Judeo-Christian tradition.

In the story of creation in Genesis, God is portrayed as creating out of nothing, by an act of grace, all that exists, and this is described as 'very good'. Given the setting of this myth of creation before the fall, the description of creation as good cannot carry at the moment of coming into existence any moral sense, since questions of morality only arise once Adam's pride has

39

been revealed through his disobedience. Also, it is hard to imagine what moral sense goodness can carry when applied to inanimate objects such as land, sea and sky, or plants and lower animals without reason and self-awareness. No, goodness has nothing here to do with morality at all.

Rather, goodness in the myth of creation means something far more akin to mutual relationship. The point being made by the story is that God looked at creation as he brought it into being and found it attractive, that he liked the look of it, that it agreed with his own sense of harmony, balance and beauty. Is this not what we would expect since creation is an act of grace, formed out of nothing, by the express will and word of God alone? If we are to call God good, then are we not describing him as the Unutterable Beauty who creates beauty, the Supreme Harmony who brings into being a harmonious order of creation, and the Perfect Love who places loveliness within the very structures of the universe? Yes, the point of the Genesis account of creation is to portray an attractive God who creates an attractive universe, in which created nature mirrors the divine nature.

Seen in this light, the goodness of creation reflects what is true about God, so that truth becomes, not an abstraction as in philosophy, but a way of describing goodness. Truth and goodness are linked thus — goodness is to do with the attractiveness of God to us, and the truth is the working out of what this means. This way of describing the meaning of goodness is stating quite simply that we find ourselves drawn to God, attracted to him, and that when we find out this truth about ourselves then we discover that we are in touch with ultimate reality, whom we call God. We believe that God exists and that he seeks to make himself known to us, and when we respond we find that we are not reaching out into a void, but returning to a loving creator who is true to his word and wants to be for us our *summum bonum*, our greatest good.

Understood thus, goodness and truth are harmoniously linked to beauty, and all three work together to reinforce the reflection of God's nature in creation. Out of such a harmony comes the orderliness of creation so that it is reliable, consistent, dependable, just like the God who created it. But such a picture, even if we occasionally catch a glimpse of its reality in visions of natural splendour and moments of harmony with the world around us, no longer holds for a fallen creation with the clarity and immediacy of the creator's original intention. Sin has brought discord into the harmony, marred the beauty, smeared truth with a lie and disordered the good order of creation, to bring chaotic elements into the world of our experience that disrupt, distort and disfigure our relationship with both the creator and the rest of his creation. Beauty and truth cease necessarily to coinhere, and goodness is overlaid with the unattractive mark of evil. The fall, so aptly named, is but a shorthand description of this process — Eve is attracted to the forbidden fruit and uses its goodness, its beauty and the truth it contains as her excuse for disobedience, and Adam consents to her decision. Between them, their pride tears apart the harmony of the created order and releases into creation the forces of evil that we call Satan, the adversary, and the struggle for man's soul begins, a struggle that we remain caught up in today as desperately and painfully as ever. Every man is indeed the Adam of his own soul, and the natural attractiveness of God to man is masked for so many still by the fear of him, felt by the first Adam and his wife when they hid from his presence among the trees of the garden, naked and trembling at the results of their presumption.

It is only at this point that goodness becomes related to morality, not out of any wish on God's part to restrict his goodness, but out of necessity, in order to restore creation to good order through the painful process of bringing into line the disorderly state of human nature, fallen into sin and into the power of the evil one.

Yet the primacy of goodness remains. Sin is not able to infect God's nature, and his continuing love for his creation sustains it in existence through his grace, moment by moment, day by day, year by year. We exist because of his graciousness towards us and his attractiveness continues to be reflected in us despite the distortions of sin and the influence of Satan. Sin is a parasite, living off the good tissues of creation, and God's responsibility for sin lies not only in his gift of the will to mankind, but in his decision to keep creation in existence after the fall. If he were to cease to love us, we would cease to be, but although this would destroy evil, it would also destroy us. Therefore, God maintains his love towards us by continuing to create us good, takes the burden of ultimate responsibility for sin upon his own shoulders, and carries that burden to Calvary. God's response to our sin is not to reject us but to draw even closer to us in Jesus his Son, and to reverse the fall by a new creation whose loving obedience, even under suffering and temptation, triumphs over evil and brings us deliverance. The risen Christ vindicates his Father's love for creation by offering us new life in him.

The birth, life, death and resurrection of Christ is God's response to the moral responsibility that he shoulders for creation, and the loving obedience of Christ the Son to his Father effects the redemption the Father desires, to fulfil his commitment to us. But what of us? How is our responsibility before God for the misuse of our wills and the abuse of our nature to be expressed?

It is not enough for us to see God as our creator, a nature deity concerned solely with the natural order of goodness. Our sin has shattered that simplicity. Our response requires us to see him as one who is firm in his goodness, sure in his love, opposed to evil and yet desiring our restoration. Thus, there enters into the spiritual consciousness of mankind the notions of right and wrong, justice and mercy, faith and unbelief, truth and falsehood. We develop a conscience, albeit a primitive and imperfect one. Man becomes aware that he is alienated from his environment, from his fellow human beings and from God, and that to approach God in trembling and fear requires at the same time seeking to live once again in harmony with the rest of creation. So it is that righteousness — right relationships — become integral to the Old Testament understanding of the life of faith. We have needed to prepare ourselves, as individuals and as a race, as best we can for the coming of Christ, by developing a moral order in society that will at least hold in check the grosser consequences of sin, even if we cannot eradicate the sin itself. We find ourselves helpless in the power of the evil one, even while our aspirations soar towards a moral reordering of ourselves and our society, and we fall down in penitence before God seeking his forgiveness and his help.

It is to answer those supplications of every generation that God sent his only Son to bring us healing, deliverance, room to live again for God. It is in Christ that we find ourselves restored to the good life, and discover in him the new creation, our eyes opened to the creation as God sees it. Furthermore, he offers us not just the restoration of the old, but because God in Christ has bound himself more closely to us than before, he offers us a further bond with himself than the one he offered to Adam — in Christ, we can find union with God in the vision of his glory. His goodness is triumphant over sin because his goodness is greater than our sin and has paid the price upon the cross. The moral goodness of God lies ultimately in his willingness to suffer in us and for us and to go on loving us even to the point of sacrifice, and this he achieves once for all in Christ. So it is that the Church, recognizing the irony of her proclamation, as she sings the paschal praises of Christ, refers to Adam's sin as *felix culpa*, happy fault, because of the greatness of the deliverance from that fault wrought by the death and resurrection of God's Son.

The life of faith cannot be divorced from the necessity to reorder our lives around the obedience of Christ and the sacrifice that this entails. Following Christ contains the demand for moral reform, the reshaping of our character into his likeness. To do otherwise is to seek to possess Christ without a participation in his sacrifice, to seek the benefits of his redeeming work without bearing the burden of our own responsibility for sin in our own lives. Therefore, faith is the spur to the costly work of reformation of character, done not primarily for our own sakes, but out of devotion to God and to his goodness and love.

Such a desire will bring us to suffering, to deprivation, to self-denial and to pain. It will cause us to embrace the way of the cross as the means of moral improvement. There will be times of agony alone in the garden of Gethsemane within our own conscience, when the prayer, 'Not my will, but thine be done', becomes our only guard against temptation and relapse. And choices once made are found to be required of us over and over again as sin is rooted out, first on the surface of our lives, and then more and more deeply from the hidden secret places of our personality and our will.

There will be times when our prayer becomes so painful and so feeble that we fear that we are failing, or worse, that God does not care. Such emotions reflect rather the tragic extent to which sin has entwined its tentacles around our innermost being. The ultimate temptation is to deny God's goodness because of the pain and suffering that come on all who travel any distance in their pilgrimage of faith.

The saints bear unanimous witness that this is Satan's last and most deadly attempt to deceive us, by tempting us to despair, to believe that the God who creates and redeems us is in fact capable of rejecting us as unattractive to him, and does so by making himself unattractive to us. The temptation is to reject the goodness of God as a fraud because our hearts are in pain, whereas the truth is that the pain derives from the fact that we have yet to learn how to open our hearts adequately to receive the full measure of love that God wishes to pour upon us. It is our sin that restricts and constrains our hearts, and so often the pain we feel is a God-given sign that there is more to his goodness than we have yet discovered or been prepared to risk discovering by repentance and amendment of life.

Seen in these terms, suffering and even death become part of the goodness of God. Both have been carried in the body of Jesus to Calvary, and in him both can be carried in our bodies as part of our way of the cross. Suffering springs from the mystery of evil and from our discipleship. That which is involuntary and mysterious derives largely from the finitude and the imperfection of creation as it is and reminds us of the human cost to Jesus of our redemption. Embraced as a means of sharing a little of his physical, intellectual, emotional and spiritual suffering, such experience can be counted as given to us for our good to be a means of grace, of growing in awareness of how much we depend upon the goodness of God for survival. That which is chosen as part of discipleship brings us close to the person of Christ, because, like him in the garden, we are seeking the Father's will and choosing the path of obedience by denying ourselves and paying the price of resisting evil. Such suffering may drive a wedge between our awareness of God's presence and the fact that he remains with us — spiritual dereliction is part of crucifixion — but we press on, believing in resurrection and the vindication of God's goodness within our suffering, because he has raised Jesus from the dead.

Dying is in one sense but the climax of suffering, but this negative view denies the merciful nature of death. Who in his right mind would want to live for ever in the world as it is? Only those who avoid suffering by moral cowardice and do not believe in the resurrection to eternal life could conceive of anything as dreadful as a world without death. Part of God's goodness is to have made us so that we are built not to last, so that we wear out, with the intention that, as our outer nature decays, our inner nature is being renewed by his grace. Death is a good friend whose hand guides us through the door of time into the realm of eternity and to union with God. We may fear to die because of the pain, the disorientation, the indignity, even the messiness, that dying may entail, but to fear death itself is to live every moment of one's life in terror of a certainty that common sense tells us we must face and faith teaches us to embrace for love of God. Far better to see our death as part of God's plan for us through which his goodness is revealed to us, than to shun death as a nightmare we could stop if only we were able to find some way of waking up.

So, for the person of faith, the primacy of goodness remains from the moment of creation to the moment of union with God, and not even our old fears and terrors, struck by sin and Satan and their allies in a fallen world, suffering and death, can overcome that goodness or displace it from its sovereign place in our hearts. God's goodness has made us for himself, and come what may, we remain restless until we find our rest in him, our great good.

One further aspect of this divine goodness remains to be mentioned. This is the sacraments. Our God is not a nature deity, but creation remains good because he creates it so. God's Son takes our human nature and makes of it the means of redemption for us all. He invites us to share his life with his body, the Church, and gives us the sacraments as the way we do so. Things of the good creation — water, bread, wine, oil, human lives, anointed hands — are taken, and given to us with prayer to bring us a gift from God. They are taken from the realm of creation and given redemptive power through the action of Christ in his Church to make them vehicles of his love and grace. God's goodness in creation and redemption meet in sacramental signs that bring our lives into direct relationship with the life of the risen and glorified Christ.

But these good things of creation are not always taken as they are made by God — for some, such as bread and wine, man's labour is there also, teaching us that all that we are and do is to come under the yoke of Christ. With the water of Baptism, however, the contrast is clear — God's goodness in pure water is a sign of his free and unmerited love towards us. Without any work on our part, he provides the sacrament of our initiation into the body of Christ so that through his grace alone we find redemption and new life in Christ.

As we ponder the meaning of the sacrament of Baptism and grow in the sacramental life of the Eucharist, as we find God's absolution in the sacrament of Reconciliation, and his healing peace in the Anointing of the sick, and as we ponder the significance of the sacraments of Marriage and Ordination, then we find that his goodness towards us becomes more and more focused in the person of Christ, and our understanding of creation changes from that of a good world seen through our eyes into a renewed world seen through the eyes of Christ. What begins as a natural sign of God's goodness to us, as we start to walk in the way of faith, becomes more and more the consummation of God's goodness towards us — creation, transfigured from within through the death and resurrection of Christ, redeemed and presented to us as a sacramental sign of his goodness to be enjoyed and offered back to God in gratitude for all that he has done for us in Christ.

Conversion to Christ brings us into a realization, however small and unformed, that we depend upon God utterly and completely for our well-being and our purpose in life and that we rely upon his goodness to draw us to himself, to maintain that well-being even in the midst of adversity, and to fulfil that purpose for our life which we see lies in him. With this impetus of grace within us, our response is to give ourselves with enthusiasm to his service, and it is to a consideration of that enthusiasm that we now turn.

FIVE

Godly Enthusiasm

One of the joyful fantasies of youth is that we shall change the world, by stamping our mark upon it. Causes are embraced; rallies supported; views held with fierce fervour; compromise is a dirty word; enthusiasm is the hallmark of sincerity. And what is true of young people (or older people with new convictions) espousing secular causes, is equally true of Christians new to faith. Their experience is often literally enthusiastic, that is, of being filled with God. Conversion, whatever form it takes, usually produces a keen and vehement response to the grace of God. Like Jehu, hot from his anointing as king of Israel, the new convert 'drives furiously' for the Lord, and can be a very uncomfortable companion for those of us who have held the faith with varying degrees of fidelity for many years. We may discover ourselves under the close scrutiny of the convert's eye and be found wanting. Perhaps we have compromised too much with sin, become conformed without noticing to the world, supped too often with the devil, and our conscience is pricked by the enthusiasm, the conviction and the dedication of the newcomer. Yet, perhaps we may feel also that he is being just a little unfair, perhaps too harsh, presuming to judge, a little short on prudence and charity, and that not all grey areas are untenable.

Enthusiasm has its place and purpose in God's scheme of things, but it is a specific place, with a real but limited purpose, intended to produce tangible but only preliminary changes in the person on fire for the Lord. It cannot, of itself, produce the end that we seek, union with God, but it does play a valuable and indispensable part in pointing the convert in the right direction and enabling him to take his first steps along the mystic road.

The purpose of enthusiasm is that it turns conversion into a living reality. When we come to faith, we need to express that faith. This need is partly because we desire to seek God's will and to do it. We wish to become disciples of Christ and enthrone him in our hearts and minds as Saviour and Lord, giving ourselves to him as his servants. We desire to show our love for him, both to him and to the world around us, so that others may see what we have found and hopefully wish to give themselves to Christ also. Conversion generates in the soul of the new believer an enthusiasm for service and for mission. But this need to express our faith also comes partly from the immaturity of our conviction. We are new to faith and we need to convince ourselves that the change we claim to have overtaken us is in fact real. Therefore we give ourselves to the work, not only out of love for Christ, but also out of personal necessity. We must prove to ourselves that what we have so confidently claimed to be true is genuine — and that it works. Practical changes and achievements are looked for in ourselves to demonstrate that we have not allowed a fantasy to take over our lives.

To anyone who considers the matter calmly, there is much that is selfish and self-regarding in conversion and the enthusiasm for God that follows, but this does not invalidate either the conversion itself or its consequences. All motivation is mixed this side of heaven, and God is able to use our weaknesses, our need, even our sin, as an agent for good. We do not attain to perfection in one step, but make progress by taking many steps forward in faith over a considerable period of time. Therefore, we must expect that such steps, especially in the initial stages, are faltering and uncertain, perhaps not well-directed even when well-intentioned, and unlikely to be entirely altruistic. Love for God and love of self remain intertwined in our hearts, and our enthusiasm springs from both. We have moved only one step, namely, from loving ourselves for our own sake towards loving God for our own sake — there is still much to be discovered and applied.

Yet, this one step is a great step forward. Enthusiasm is not to be despised because it is imperfect in love and selflessness. It is a step in the right direction towards the godly life. What it requires is a harnessing of its energy and constant checking of its tendency to recklessness and harshness. To help us do this we need to examine the nature and direction of the change that conversion is bringing about in the soul, and to see how the development produced by that change is potentially capable of even greater things once it matures.

Conversion is from pride and unbelief to faith and humility — or rather to the beginnings of faith and the desire for humility, struggling to overcome the grip of pride and the habit of unbelief. Enthusiasm gives us the driving power to enlist in this struggle and to use the grace God has given us to engage in spiritual warfare. The convert is not a victor but a combatant and his fight 'against sin, the world and the devil' is waged in deadly earnest.

So, the first point is that conversion is from pride and unbelief, so that we struggle to become free from their hold over us. The convert, fired with enthusiasm for God, renounces his old sins — he repents and vows to amend his life after the pattern of Christ. In the first heady days, he is swept along by his experience of grace and effects mighty changes in his life. He often believes that what he has achieved constitutes a decisive break with the past and that his steps are irrevocably pointed in the direction of holiness. His new faith will surely be sufficient to save him from any temptation to revert to his former ways and commit those old sins again.

Sadly, it is only very rarely so. Usually the habit of sin remains a strong influence, an undertow of disorderly desiring that disrupts the progress made, showing up the achievements gained as superficial. We have relied too much on our own strength and we find ourselves humiliated before God — and our own pride — when the fall occurs. The truth is that solid progress from sin to goodness, from vice to virtue, comes only through suffering.

Enthusiasm will show us what it can be like to live resistant to our besetting temptations and momentarily free from the habits of sin which they lead us to commit; but it does not have the inner strength to help us to hold fast to our convictions and resist those temptations indefinitely. We are relying too much on our own strength, and too little on God's grace. And so we fall and we suffer.

This is a moment of great danger. What seemed to produce a great change in our life is discovered to be weak and vulnerable in the face of our sinful desires. The temptation is to blame God and to doubt his grace and his power. The inexperience of the convert in the ways of God may lead him into three false attitudes.

One is the reaction that God has let him down or that God does not exist. This is in effect the temptation to unbelief, to abandon our new-found faith as a delusion and a lie, to react as violently against the idea of God as we had reacted in favour before. Among many of the most hardened unbelievers are those who have tried religion and found it failed them. Put in these terms we can see that such a reaction is the product of making God in the mirror-image of our own needs and inadequacies and then finding that our needs and inadequacies, being real, are stronger than the mirror-image which is a product of our fantasy.

The high 'drop-out' rate of converts from certain

types of churches and rallies which use 'born again' criteria must raise serious doubts about, not only the legitimacy of the method, but also the inadequacy of the pastoral care exercised afterwards. To presume that the convert has spiritual maturity because of his conversion experience is not ony foolish but destructive. The new Christian needs to be nurtured in the faith and directed in the spiritual life, or else he is highly likely to fall prey to precisely those forces for evil which he had thought so decisively defeated in the moment of ecstatic conversion.

Another false attitude is hypocrisy. This temptation is to cover up our relapses into former ways by pretending that it does not matter — or even worse, does not happen. Hypocrisy whispers to us that the show of faith is all that matters and that provided we present the correct image of the good Christian, our private falls can be contained and rendered harmless. Thus it becomes habitual to refer to sin as something in the past, before conversion, and grace as our present state, since conversion. Jesus reserves his severest condemnation for such an attitude, pointing out that hypocrisy never deceives others for long but shows itself as a division within the person between what he says and what he does. The hypocrite is the one who condemns others of the same thing that he himself is content to practise in private. There is no integrity.

Once hypocrisy eats into the soul it begins to react in a divisive way — the divided person within sets out to divide the Church also. Other Christians are separated out into sheep and goats. The judgement of Christ is usurped by the hypocrite, and he declares who is saved and who are damned, who is holy and who are in the grip of Satan. The history of communities based on enthusiasm is one of divisiveness, as 'holiness groups' reject and condemn those with whom they disagree. The competitive spirit replaces the spirit of forgiveness and love as the means open to the hypocrite of justifying his inner contradiction. God becomes a weapon wielded by the hypocrite to bolster his own pride, whereas his only salvation lies along the opposite road of repentance, forgiveness, restoration to grace and love in the fellowship of faith.

The third reaction is guilt, a sense of burning shame that having professed so much, spoken so mightily, claimed for oneself such progress, we have betrayed our God and ourselves. Many Christians are riddled with guilt, and they cope with it by either losing sight of God's forgiveness through concentrating on his unapproachable holiness, or by plunging themselves into punishing 'good works' that hopefully will merit, if not God's forgiveness then at least his understanding and mercy. Unfortunately, the temptation to sin is reinforced by both attitudes, because each draws attention in different ways to ourselves and our fallen condition.

To place all of one's attention on the transcendence of God is to press down our sinful condition even further into the mire and debase our humanity as unworthy of him — the goodness of creation and the fact of the incarnation are played down in favour of God's moral indignation and a vision of the cross as punishment and retribution.

To take on good works as a way of expiating our sins is to punish ourselves for them, and so, by the very punishment, keep our sins before our eyes. Furthermore, when such good works take the form of a vocation such as ordination to the priesthood, entering a religious community or joining a caring profession, then our goodness, even holiness, in the sight of others, is a further turn of the screw of our self-torture.

The incidence of mental breakdown among enthusiastic converts who have failed to reconcile their tendency to sin with God's continuing desire to grant them forgiveness is a tragic witness to the limitations of conversion and enthusiasm. At its worst, the internal stress turns outwards in a combination of extreme confessions of sin that seem to others to be exaggerated, or even attention-seeking, and harshness towards others who do not have the need to punish themselves in the same way or to the same degree as the tormented soul who cannot find release from guilt. Ironically, extremes of Catholic and Protestant devotion link hands here, inflicting the same severe psychological damage on their disciples.

And when the tendency to unbelief, hypocrisy and guilt combine, then indeed is fulfilled in the convert the parable of Jesus about the demon gathering together others worse than himself and going back to his former home to find it swept and prepared for his return. For some converts, their last state does become worse than their first because the God they claim to worship, love and serve has become demonic, through their own failure to understand and accept the Gospel.

The antidote to this triple poison is the acceptance of suffering after the example of Christ. He tells us clearly that we must take up our cross and follow him, that the cost of discipleship must be taken into account when we convert. Of course, it is impossible to make an accurate assessment of that cost before we begin to walk the way of the cross. All that we are called to recognize is that suffering will come and that Christ will be walking with us, falling beneath the cross when we fall and helping us to stand once more as we struggle to rise again under its weight. Is Jesus our Simon of Cyrene or are we his? It is usually impossible to tell, because the truth is that both insights are true. Our cross is his cross, and his suffering redeems our pain.

The enthusiasm of the convert may give him a glimpse of life free from sin, but it will not sustain that glimpse so that it becomes a way of life. What is needed here is the reformation of character after the pattern of Christ, centred on obedience to the will of God. Our will is to be conformed to Christ's will, so that our life imitates his life. For this to happen motivation is all important. We must desire this change because we see it as for our own good.

Here, enthusiasm plays its positive part because the glimpse given of life lived in conformity to Christ causes the convert to realize that the faith he has embraced has practical benefits. Being Christlike is possible, albeit, at first, for only short periods. A vision of holiness opens our eyes, adding the virtue of hope to that of our faith and exciting our love for God to greater depths than conversion itself produced. A threefold cord of faith, hope and love is beginning to entwine itself about our soul, enclosing it in its new found desire for God.

For the sake of meeting that desire with possession, we are called by Christ to renounce our past sins, to repent and to amend our lives after his example, as the first step in a series of steps towards gaining our heart's desire. This reformation of character is not achieved in a moment, as we know to our cost, but it is achieved sufficiently over a period of time for us to notice the difference that conversion has initiated. By straightforward acts of the will, strengthened and inspired by the grace of God, most of the coarsest and peripheral sins to which we are prone can be eradicated. In particular, sins of word and action, or sins of omission, can be largely put on one side and the opposite virtues practised with increasing reliability.

This is especially true of acts of covetousness, sloth, greed and lust, the carnal and physical sins that move around our animal appetites and the cruder aspects of our selfishness. But it is much harder to make progress with pride, envy and anger, those sins of the human spirit that rise from our self-assertion, our worldly identity and our aggression towards others. These latter are more deeply rooted in our sinfulness and yield only slowly to the grace of God, because we fear to lose them lest we lose the very framework that defines ourselves in a fallen world. To make real progress with these sins we need to secure first our identity with Christ.

Sins of thought in all these categories are more difficult than those of word and action, largely because our desiring is disorderly at the level of our minds long after we have brought our physical nature under reasonable control.

Also, sinful habits are more difficult to reverse into good habits than a once only act of sin. Vices yield reluctantly to the practice of the opposite virtues, whereas an exceptional act, even if premeditated, is less likely to plant itself so insidiously in the soul and can be rooted out quite easily with a definite act of contrition and a setting of the will against a repetition of the sin. It is precisely constant repetition of a sin that weakens the will and produces a vice, and such vices are clear indications of aspects of our character which are vulnerable to temptation and will almost certainly be the areas of major conflict against sin for the rest of our lives. One of the values of being regular in the use of the sacrament of Reconciliation is the recognition, that comes from going to confession, where one's strengths and weaknesses lie, and therefore, where the struggle is likely to be most wounding and most costly.

To make progress here in this work of reformation of character is to suffer many set-backs, many disappointments, often appalling insights into how deeply penetrating our sin remains in the deepest recesses of our soul, and how much we rely on our vices for pleasure and purpose. The suffering here is intense because it carries with it three aspects, which we need to recognize if we are to progress.

The first aspect of this suffering under sin is that it is

humiliating. As the grace of God brings us forgiveness and power to amend our lives after the pattern of Christ, it also brings us awareness of just how strong the grip of sin upon us remains; that there is still a long way to go before we shall be Christlike. The beneficial aspect of this realization is that it causes us to recognize our total dependence upon God and his love for us as the necessary precondition for any progress at all. We need him to remain faithful to us, hopeful about us and loving towards us, if we are to grow towards him in faith, hope and love. Also, humiliation before God is a necessary preliminary to the development of humility, the very fount of all virtue and antidote to pride and all its dependent vices. This humility is like good soil, humus in which the seed of faith will grow strongly to yield one hundredfold by the grace of God and our own surrender of self-will for God's will. In a strange way, we are not to assert our will for ourselves but for God, and to find in doing so that what we will for God turns out to be for our own ultimate good.

The second aspect of this suffering is that rooting out our sin is painful, because it goes against ingrained habits of a lifetime. Other people may look at us with surprise or disgust to see us changed, and may reject us as unbalanced or no longer the person we once were. Virtue may be its own reward, but so too is vice. Also, resisting temptation when it comes may cost us dear in terms of effort of the will. To be sorely tempted is to be torn apart physically and psychologically, often at our weakest point, and Satan knows only too well how to press home his advantage when spiritual exhaustion lowers our resistance. Such spiritual warfare wounds us all and to fall into sin in such circumstances is only damning if we lose faith and fail to turn to God for forgiveness and strength to go on again. This suffering under the duress of temptation is best seen not as our individual struggle with evil, but as part of the cosmic struggle in which the whole creation is engaged and in which God has called us to play our part. Any resistance, however feeble and fleeting, is a defeat for Satan and a share in Christ's redeeming work on the cross. When we give in to temptation and sin, then God's forgiveness is always there to bring triumph out of defeat, and to plant his peace in the midst of our warfare.

And the third aspect of this suffering is the pain of deprivation. Our sins have a familiar, perhaps comfortable, feel about them, and they are so much part of us that we rely on them more than we realize to shape and direct our lives. To reject these sins and to seek to practise the opposite virtues leaves a large emotional and intellectual void within us. We are deprived of the consolation and comforts of our sins and find ourselves yearning for the old familiar ways. The new life of faith is hard to accept because it is so unfamiliar and makes demands upon us that before we would not have considered possible, let alone congenial. The example of Christ is not immediately attractive to our disorderly desires, even if our new-found faith sees it so. We are divided within by the difference between what faith wants of us and what our instincts cry out for. The new way seems so bleak, so self-denying, so rejecting of what others take for granted as natural and therefore in their terms right.

The demand of Christ upon the convert causes this deprivation to be endured for the sake of gaining a better way of life, but the cost of discipleship, of leaving all to follow Christ, is paid dearly in the first stages of the life of faith. Until the convert has grown used to and accepted this deprivation as a settled state of affairs the benefits will not appear, and the suffering experienced can only be borne in faith, believing and trusting that the promise of Christ that his yoke is easy and his burden is light will come true for him in due time.

Yet, difficult as it will be, we are called to surrender the past, exorcizing it of its power to control us by repentance, the discovery of forgiveness and the firm purpose of amendment of life by the grace of God. We are to desire the virtues of Christ, chiefly among them humility, meekness and love, and to grow away from self-control towards God-control in which we find ourselves willingly surrendering our lives into his hands, to make of us what he desires for us, not what we seek for ourselves. Here we seek to imitate Christ, who prayed, 'Not my will, but thine be done', so that the garden of Gethsemane becomes for us the place of return to the new garden of Eden, where Christ is all in all to us.

This bleak diagnosis of the first steps of the convert's life in Christ is however only half the story. By itself, such experience would deter even the most enthusiastic follower. The truth is that the new Christian is a tender plant in need of attention, and there need to be compensations from God if he is to make the effort required to surrender his past.

At this point, we need to remind ourselves that God's grace turns our weaknesses into strengths, and in this case the weakness which God uses to our advantage is our dependency upon pleasure. He has created us as desiring creatures, with a will to seek and to find happiness, satisfaction and fulfilment. This desiring aspect of our nature is good because it is given to us by God so that we might 'feel after him and find him'. Without this desiring will within us union with God would be impossible.

However, our sin has distorted this desiring and diverted it into other channels, so that we seek lesser goods and often evil itself to be the object of our desires, and we bend our wills to find pleasure in them and not in the living God. We love what is created and even what is sinful more than we love the Creator and his will for us. The pleasure principle has become for us a snare rather than a help in our quest for personal happiness and mature fulfilment.

But God takes this misdirected good that lies within us and has become a weakness, and makes of it a strength. His grace leads us to find spiritual pleasures following conversion. These spiritual pleasures usually include a new sense of closeness to God, a satisfaction in spending time in prayer, emotional and physical delight in worship, especially in receiving Holy Communion and finding forgiveness in the sacrament of Reconciliation, much joy in reading the Scriptures and other spiritual books, a real sense of fulfilment in sharing the company of other Christians, an intellectual satisfaction from studying the faith and learning more of Christ, a great sense of directed energy in the pursuit of good works, and so on.

For some, vocations may be presented to them as ways of seeking God's will, and the call embraced with joy and enthusiasm (sometimes, however, unfortunately misdirected so that the vocation either fades or is not accepted as authentic by the Church). For others, particular gifts of the Spirit may be given to build up the recipient. St Paul's list of enthusiastic gifts of the Spirit is reproduced among converts quite regularly, though not unfailingly. No one gift is a sign of true conversion, since the Spirit distributes to each as he wills. Indeed, the apostle is quite clear that the more spectacular gifts are given to the weaker members, who need more spiritual pleasures to sustain them in faith than the more mature among them. The Spirit gives spiritual pleasures according to our need and for the common good of the body of Christ, and these two principles govern his choice of gifts for us. We should beware of using psychological pressure upon others to force them to fake spiritual gifts which God has not given them. At this point what should be helpful becomes harmful, and what is believed to be spiritual good is in fact demonic in its origins.

However, for most there are no spectacular spiritual gifts, but much more the ordinary gifts of the Spirit that bind Christians together in the body of Christ, so that the Church reflects and presents Christ to the world through evangelism, social concern, prayer and worship, a common life lived in harmony and peace, and sound teaching. In these areas the convert can make significant contributions which are both personally satisfying and assist the work of the whole Church.

But no matter what gifts are endowed upon the convert by the Spirit, all are intended to bring spiritual pleasure, and to encourage him to maintain the faith he has embraced, as he fights to surrender the past into the hands of God and to reform his life to that of Christ's. The suffering of that struggle is compensated with spiritual pleasures, so that what is endured for the sake of Christ becomes worthwhile. The convert is still weak in resolution and, without God's concern for redirecting his desire for pleasure into spiritual paths, there would be little progress and possibly even relapse into unbelief.

Of course, although the gifts of the Spirit vary from one person to another in accordance with individual need and the common good, growth in the fruit of the Spirit is incumbent upon us all. This is another positive side of the struggle to be Christlike, and indeed, the underlying motivation for pursuing virtue rather than vice. The amendment of life which leads to growth in virtue springs properly from a desire to bring forth the fruit (not fruits) of the Spirit, namely, love, joy, peace, patience, kindness, goodness, faithfulness, gentleness, temperance. All of these are one fruit, to be sought by all as the means of developing a balanced life of virtue. Without them, virtue becomes a tyrannical, obsessive life-denying set of rules that destroy human freedom, because it is self-imposed. With the fruit of the Spirit, virtue becomes a lovely and gracious reflection in the believer's life of the Christ who is our pattern and our reward.

These various spiritual pleasures work together to lift the new Christian up from self-absorption with sin and the past, and set his feet on the road to union with God. Like Christ, he is prepared to endure the cross, despising the shame, for the joy that is set before him. And like St Paul, he can cry out with conviction, 'I have been crucified with Christ. It is no longer I who live but Christ who lives in me. And the life I now live in the flesh I live by faith in the Son of God who loved me and sacrificed himself for me.'

It is to these spiritual pleasures, so necessary and so valuable, which bring so much to the convert, that we must now turn in detail, with particular reference to prayer and meditation.

SIX

Sound Words

To pray is to be human and to be human is to pray. But the grace of conversion moves a natural and instinctive response to unknown divinity into desire for a supernatural and conscious relationship with the God and Father of our Lord Jesus Christ. Prayer ceases to be a casual, often thoughtless, activity which bears no necessary connection with belief, and becomes a chosen, deliberate, willed expression of faith in the goodness of God. We seek him because we wish to entrust our lives to his safe keeping and to bend our wills to his purposes. And so we start to pray in a way unknown to us before, a way that presupposes a developing friendship with God in which disclosure occurs on both sides — we reveal ourselves to him as he reveals himself to us, or rather, we find ourselves revealed to ourselves, as he reveals himself to us and we see in him our true selves, reflected in the person of Jesus Christ. Through this disclosure, the grace of God enters our lives and gives us the incentive and the strength to grow in the Christian life and to surrender ourselves more fully into his hands.

Such praying is begun by the convert with enthusiasm, and becomes regular through perseverance, long after enthusiasm has waned. The habit of daily prayer develops as the framework of a prayerful life, focused on God and centred in Jesus Christ. We lift up our hearts and minds at certain times and in particular places as a sign that all times and all places are dedicated to prayer. As with love between two people when moments of meeting transform the rest of the day, so times of prayer transfigure all times and all places with the remembrance of God's presence and our devotion to him. And just as the failure to give time and attention to human love raises a question mark over our declarations that we are committed, so we may reasonably query our own commitment to loving God if we cannot give to him that regular undivided attention which daily prayer requires. It is a lesson in discipleship to pray habitually, a sacrificing of self-interest and self-will in favour of the beloved, which carries the authentic marks of Christ's cross found in daily faithfulness.

Also, like all other new relationships, the means of communication that we rely on most to make ourselves known is words. We speak to one another as the primary means open to us of sharing what is in our hearts and in our minds. Gestures help but need to be articulated. Therefore, words and actions combine to express our love for God, our desire to serve him, our concern for others, the many sides of our growing experience of the life of faith. Such verbalizing of the relationship is our attempt to convey to God the place he now holds in our lives as our creator and redeemer.

Therefore, the key to this early prayer — and indeed to all prayer — is appreciation. We value what we appreciate; we recognize the worth of what we count as our treasure. And when God becomes that treasure, then we worship him first and foremost by expressing our appreciation of him. This appreciation is commonly called thanksgiving, and takes us to the heart of the prayer of Jesus himself who regularly gave thanks.

But the thanksgiving of Jesus is not the sort of grace before meals that passes for thanksgiving, even though his thanks to God were often made in the context of a meal. Rather, he thanked God for his creative and redemptive acts, so that the food and drink shared at table became for him and his disciples sustenance received in remembrance of God's love for them. This is the origin of the Eucharist, in which the Church thanks God for creation and redemption in and through Jesus Christ and does so in remembrance of him over bread and wine. But it is also the inspiration of our daily prayer in which thanksgiving rehearses those same acts of God as the basis of our faith and the means through which we are reconciled to God and receive his grace into our lives. Our prayer is eucharistic because we appreciate the value of what God has done for us in Christ, whom we worship as our heart's desire, the Lamb worthy of praise and honour and glory and blessing.

It is impossible to over-emphasize the central importance of thanksgiving to the Christian life. The difference between faith and unbelief is demonstrated most clearly by the willingness to give thanks, and knowing to whom that thanks should be rendered. Indeed one of the basic dilemmas of the unbeliever is finding a suitable recipient for his thanksgiving, on those rare occasions when he feels thankful. To put the matter tritely, we are discussing the difference between being grateful for a cup half-full and complaining about a cup half-empty. The facts remain the same, it is the disposition towards them that makes the difference. This is the reason why thanksgiving, gratitude, appreciation form the heart of our prayer — because it reflects our faith.

This thanksgiving is primarily for what God has done for us in and through his Son Jesus Christ. Only secondarily is it thanksgiving for particular blessings recently received. Sometimes the latter do become uppermost in our minds — for example, on the birth of a child or for passing an examination — but this should be exceptional, not the rule.

There are two reasons for this. To count one's particular blessings as the first cause for thanksgiving can easily lead to a 'cupboard-love' for God in which we are increasingly dependent on 'hand-outs'. This undermines the saving works of Christ as our chief joy and encourages us to misunderstand suffering or deprivation when they come. Only Christ's work lasts; all else passes away. It is wise to cling to Christ alone and not to any created good that happens to come into our life through the grace of God. To do otherwise is to develop the wrong perspective upon God's love for us and to give undue prominence to transient blessings which we are required to appreciate only in the context of God's love in Christ, and even then as lesser goods which we are not to seek or hold on to when they are given. All things that are good are to be surrendered for the sake of the good that Jesus has won for us.

Secondly, to concentrate on particular individual blessings encourages egoism. It strengthens the self by imagining that such-and-such a blessing has been given to us because we are worthy of it. We imagine that God has chosen well, because we can really use what is given. This is especially insidious when the use to which we put the blessing is a spiritual one, so that God is consciously served through it. The truth is that particular blessings are freely given by God out of his sovereign love and we have no merit before him that can gain any purchase upon his grace. He gives as he wills, not as we wish or imagine he should. All comes from him and if the gift is well used it is because he works through us with his gift to enable us to respond. Therefore, to accept humbly and to receive with a sense of dependence is the necessary disposition before thanksgiving for any particular blessing can be properly offered. And then, only on the understanding that the Lord gives, and the Lord takes away, and in both the Lord is to be thanked. 'Till death us do part' is the rule of Christian marriage, and it applies spiritually to all of God's particular blessings, that a time may well come when he parts us from them so that we have to die to them in order to live for God.

So, the thanksgiving which comes first is for the general work of Jesus Christ, that has brought God's blessing upon all of creation, and only secondly, within that general blessing, humble appreciation of particular gifts received individually. We make this thanksgiving with words that express our gratitude to God for all aspects of Christ's work, for the work of creation in and through the word, for the word made flesh as Jesus of Nazareth, for his life and ministry as the Christ, for his teaching, his miracles, his example of truly human life, for his Baptism, for the last supper and his gift of the Eucharist, for his passion and crucifixion, for his resurrection from the dead and ascension into heaven, for his reign in glory as King, for the gift of the Spirit, for the Church as the Body of Christ, for the means of grace, for the saints, for the hope of eternal life, for the promise of union with God in Christ.

Here we have in outline the content of our thanksgiving. But such a list contains far too great a vision of God's love and goodness to be encompassed in one act of thanksgiving in prayer. Therefore, we break down the material into manageable sections to enable us to respond to different aspects of Christ's work at different times. Of course, we are looking at facets of one diamond and the brilliance of one facet continues to be illuminated by the light coming from the others. No one aspect of Christ's work stands alone or apart from the others — it is all of a piece, and the division of the work into smaller units is necessary to meet our inadequacy at this stage of our prayer, not because it reflects the mind of Christ.

So it is that the Church's calendar with its seasons of the year, starting with Advent and Christmas and working through Lent to Holy Week and Easter, on to Pentecost, Trinity Sunday and Corpus Christi, and then forward to Advent again via a consideration of the life and teaching of Christ, gives us a useful framework to apply to this central act of thanksgiving in daily prayer. Here the Church's prayer and ours meet in a common appreciation of what God in Christ has done for us.

But it may be that we shall need our own framework of thanksgiving to supplement the liturgical calendar. Therefore, many people find it helpful to associate the days of the week with different aspects of Christ's work. One useful pattern is as follows:

Sunday:	Creation and providence.
	The resurrection of Christ and our re-creation in him.
Monday:	The incarnation: Jesus, the Word made flesh.
	God with us.
Tuesday:	The life and teaching of Jesus as the Christ.
	The Bible and the teaching of the Church.
Wednesday:	The gift of the Spirit.
	My Baptism and Confirmation.
Thursday:	The ascension of Christ.
	The Eucharist.
Friday:	The cross of Christ.
	The forgiveness of sins, reconciliation with God.
Saturday:	The saints and the angels.
	The promise of eternal life and union with God.

Out of such a scheme of thanksgiving come other aspects of our relationship with God, now to find their expression in our prayer. These will vary from day to day, but should all be present to some degree over a reasonable period of time. They reflect a rounded development that is sane and sensible and avoids idiosyncratic tendencies. These other constituents are adoration, penitence and intercession.

Adoration flows from thanksgiving as our soul glimpses a vision of God as he is through the work that he has done for us in Christ. God's love is the spring of his action, and when we appreciate his work we may see momentarily the glory that lies behind the activity. So we respond by being drawn away from thanksgiving into fleeting moments of wonder when we desire God for his own sake, and not for what he has done for us, and we express our adoration in simple and unaffected cries of love and devotion. We are carried away by the Unutterable Beauty whose grace fills the world, and we lose our hearts to his divine splendour.

But adoration has no sense of discrimination. Left to itself, it will bind our hearts to whatever our souls desire, and in a fallen world it is easy for adoration to bind us to inadequate or even evil objects of devotion. What we do, in effect, is to make the object of our devotion our god, and to offer to that god a parody of true religion. At one level, there is little harm in this — young men fall in love with unsuitable girls and young girls adore unsatisfactory young men, and soon learn, through suffering or disappointment, to temper their impulses with discrimination. But if the adoration persists and becomes a settled habit, then it becomes a source of sin in the life of its victim. So it is that some become power-crazed, covetous, miserly, lecherous, gluttonous, coarsening their nature by losing their wills to inadequate objects of devotion.

Therefore, adoration should always be informed by thanksgiving, and should arise out of it. To seek to adore too soon is to run the risk of adoring an image or impression of God, made more in our own likeness to meet our needs, than in the likeness of Christ and his reflection of the Father's nature.

The ingredient of penitence arises naturally out of thanksgiving as the work of Christ presented to us in thanksgiving causes us to reflect upon our love returned for God's love to us. Our sins become not simply moral faults against the law of Christ but denials of the power of his love to make us Christlike. And so our penitence becomes less a stern self-accusation that we hope will drive us to steel our wills to do better, and turns more and more towards a sorrow for sin that arises out of our love for Christ and our deep desire to love him better in the future. It is not that morality means less to us, but that the true motivation, that of love for God, transforms morality into more than keeping laws and commandments.

So it may be that what begins as a daily examination of conscience becomes in time a sense of living under the love of Christ, and the failure to be Christlike that that love reveals to us. Particular sins continue to be confessed, but no longer as our only sins, but as symptomatic of the difference between ourselves as we are and the vision of ourselves that God has for us in Christ. The particular details of our penitence become expressions of our more general sinfulness and reminders of the continuing underlying tendency within us towards sin. Thus, every element of congratulation that can so perversely infect even the most serious confession is taken away, and replaced by the humbling realization of the overwhelming extent we continue to rely upon the patience and generosity of God.

Intercession comes last because its purpose emerges from thanksgiving, adoration and penitence. Our requests for others and for ourselves are intended to present before the throne of God the petitions of a servant, whose very existence is dependent upon the love of his Lord, and whose aim in life is to serve him and to love him in return. To thank, adore and repent provides the means of seeing clearly how we and others stand in God's sight, how much he loves us and desires our good, and how that good is totally bound up with surrender to his will. To intercede prematurely may mean asking wrongly because we are not praying from that position of thankful, adoring, penitent faith.

Therefore, although intercession may contain elaborate detail about the human condition — all of which is well-known to God before we say it — that detail is an expression of our personal concern and our human anxiety and is only preliminary to the prayer itself. That prayer in the end comes down to one of three petitions — Lord have mercy; thy kingdom come; thy will be done — and to say more is ultimately unnecessary.

However, to say more is human, and at this early stage in prayer God smiles upon our intercession when it carries not only the necessary petitions, but also the burden of our human love and sorrow. The further detailing, not only of information but also of our hopes and fears, is permissible provided that we see the latter as the expression of our will but not necessarily God's. In the end, when we have said all that is in our hearts for others and for ourselves, then it is God's mercy, his kingdom and his will that we seek, remembering always that for ourselves the petition is often, 'Not my will but thine be done'.

There is one other aspect of intercession which we must consider, and that is its critical quality. When we pray for others, we are testing our own integrity. How we behave towards others in practice is the criterion of the authenticity of our intercession. We cannot pray for peace without being peacemakers ourselves; we cannot seek God's mercy when we are merciless; we cannot ask for the coming of the kingdom in righteousness if we support injustice, intolerance or oppression; we cannot plead that God's will be done in the lives of others when we refuse to change, remaining self-willed and disobedient in the face of God's call to follow Christ. Intercession and practical carrying of the cross are two sides of one coin, the cost of discipleship.

To help to achieve this integrity, we need to return to

the dependence of intercession upon thanksgiving. Asking flows from knowing and appreciating, and therefore it can be useful to relate particular areas of intercession to particular areas of thanksgiving on a weekly plan. Obviously, certain people and certain concerns present us with a daily duty to pray for them, e.g. family, the government, the parish. But over and above these, a parallel scheme of intercession to the one set out for thanksgiving can prove valuable because it relates the two aspects of prayer directly. Thus, a suggested outline of intercession would be:

Sunday: For the right use of the world's resources.
For international reconciliation and co–operation.
For a deeper affirmation of the resurrection in my life.
For peace with God.

Monday: For my daily work; for attention to Christ's presence in my place of work; for my colleagues.
For a sense of 'God with us' during the day.

Tuesday: For bishops and all who teach the faith, especially N our bishop.
For my parish study groups; for my own study of the faith.
For schools, universities and all who teach in them.

Wednesday: For renewal of the Church in the life of the Spirit.
For Christian maturity.
For those preparing for Baptism and Confirmation.
For the guidance of the Spirit upon those in authority.

Thursday: For the spread of the kingdom of God;
              for the Church as the sign of that
              kingdom.
              For deeper devotion to the Eucharist and
              more faithful receiving of the Blessed
              Sacrament.
              For all priests, especially . . .
Friday: For all penitents; for those who are
              lapsed, the impenitent and indifferent.
              For those who have yet to hear the
              Gospel.
              For the sick, bereaved, especially . . .
Saturday: For perseverance in faith; for deepening
              of hope.
              For the prayers of Our Lady and all the
              saints.
              For the repose of the faithful departed,
              especially . . .
              For the consummation of all things in
              Christ.

Such an outline scheme can be adapted easily to fit the individual and should be seen as the starting point for a plan of intercession to meet our personal requirements. Obviously, some elements — perhaps most — are common to us all, but each of us will differ in the emphasis made, depending on our circumstances. But such an outline, related to a daily scheme of thanksgiving, plus those intercessions which are our daily duty, will lead us into a comprehensive and balanced pattern of prayer before God.

Two other words commonly used in discussions about prayer need to be mentioned at this stage — these are praise and worship. In fact, they contain much the same idea as thanksgiving because both are concerned also with appreciation. Praise is concerned with placing a price on God and worship is to do with expressing the worth of God. In other words, both are acts of appreciation, in which the believer states the great value that God has for him. Usually, praise and worship are terms used of corporate prayer and involve music, singing, dramatic acts of rejoicing as the Church's expression of thanksgiving, but psalms and hymns and spiritual songs can well be used by individuals in their daily prayer as a helpful contribution to their thanksgiving and often lead to a spontaneous act of adoration. Such aids should be sought and used by the beginner as a powerful means of articulating love and gratitude and joy towards God. There is within us all the influence not only of music upon the soul at the time of performance with others, but also the stirring of the soul by the recalling of the music later when alone; and this, for some people, can mean even more to them later alone than it does at the time when the offering of praise was made with the worship of the community of faith. It becomes precious because it links them with the Church at large, so that encouragement to persevere in prayer becomes almost tangible.

The development of the convert's prayer happens under the guidance of the grace of God when he co-operates in his will with the divine urging in his soul. As such it is supernatural in origin, and therefore in a fallen world, at first experienced as unnatural. By this is meant that sinful and unbelieving people do not pray in this manner, and while faith helps us to make the move in the right direction, the sin remaining within us still prevents an entirely easy and unselfconscious growth in the life of prayer. We need to apply ourselves to the task, to make a special effort to reorganize our life around prayer, and to seek the help that comes from the Christian tradition, to give us support and inspiration.

It takes time and application to establish the commitment to prayer that God requires of us and that we need for the health of our soul. Hand in hand with reformation of character after the pattern of Christ, our prayer develops through sweat and tears into a good habit, accepted and loved by the believer. But the achievement of that good habit may take many months, possibly several years, depending partly on the seriousness of the sin within us that delays reformation of life and partly on the establishment of prayer as a fixed point of entry for the grace of God into the soul. Once again, the central truth of the redemptive place of suffering in order to gain newness of life must be our guide. To build our prayer into a firm foundation for future progress means always taking up the cross in prayer at this initial stage and denying ourselves parts of our life which though perhaps good in themselves come between us and the practice of prayer. Our daily life needs to be recast around time to pray if God is to become the centre of our life, and his grace our support and stay at all times and in all places. To do this, we need useful and practical advice on how to proceed, and this advice consists of three elements — time, place, materials.

The first element, that of time, is of the essence. Unless we set aside particular times for prayer, we shall not pray. For many people this is the most difficult of all the components of the life of prayer, one which is most easily compromised. Yet without the giving of time, there is no prayer. Our decision to give time therefore may well be costly, and that in two respects.

First, there is the matter of time of day — when shall we pray. The traditional practice has been morning and evening, a pattern well suited to a settled routine of daily life with work filling the centre of the day, a short journey to and from work and a settled evening at home. In many ways, it is a rural or pre-industrial model. If that model can still be applied, then the convert need look no further, and the issue becomes one of giving up time on rising in the morning and again in

the evening before one becomes tired. Evening enter-
tainment may have to be curtailed but no serious
difficulties should arise. But if work involves lengthy
commuting or rotating shifts, or if work is later in the
day or in the evening, or this applies to other members
of the household so that the preparation of meals has to
be adjusted to allow for their work-patterns, then the
traditional model of morning and evening prayer may
prove difficult, or impossible, to apply. Fortunately, all
times are God's time, and we adjust the traditional
model to ensure that we can reliably devote the time
required. Thus, a commuter may find that lunch-time is
a good choice for prayer, but that it is necessary to get
up earlier if he is to pray before catching the train. The
child coming back from school may discover that the
best time is on arrival home, before homework is done
and the television is switched on. Each of us must find
our own time and keep it as an appointment with God
which we promise to him, knowing that keeping the
appointment will at times require costly sacrifice on our
part.

But the consideration of time also raises the question
of how long we should pray. In this matter it is wise not
to be over-ambitious. It is better to promise a short time
which we can be fairly certain of being able to give, than
to break a promise which was unrealistically presumptuous. Therefore, most people start with five minutes at
a stretch, and only when this is regularly and naturally
exceeded, extend the time to ten minutes. We do better
to discover some of the difficulties of prayer before
allowing enthusiasm to make us too bold, and therefore
time spent with little or nothing to say should be part of
our experience before we add further time to what we
have already promised. There is no merit in length of
time for its own sake — it is far more pleasing to God to
be attentive to prayer, even when it is hard, for a short
time than to fill longer periods with empty phrases,

heaped up to disguise the inner poverty of our praying. Of course, once our prayer becomes habitual we may wish to extend it considerably, and then the matter of when we pray may have to be reconsidered to take into account the length of time we wish to give to prayer.

The second element is that of place — where shall we pray. Here the unnaturalness of prayer is a vital consideration. It may be a *tour de force* to pray on a building site to the sound of pneumatic drills, but it hardly helps the average person to find daily recollection. We need to find silence and solitude, in order to give God our undivided attention to the best of our ability. Jesus talks of praying in secret in our inner chamber and perhaps for many a suitable room in the house is best. Commuters may find the office unsuitable and seek a local church open at lunch-time; shoppers may do the same in the morning or afternoon. By and large, gardens should be avoided, especially in countries of unreliable climate. Also, they are not conducive to keeping one's material in good order.

Perhaps there is no place for silence unless we create one, and this may mean turning off the television in order to be still and silent for prayer. Indeed, the practice of silence during the day by cutting out distraction and noise is an invaluable asset in preparing for prayer, because it teaches us to grow familiar with the very conditions in which prayer flourishes. However, if may be that such silence is new to us and reveals in us aspects of ourselves that we would prefer not to face. Initially many people may find silence depressing or frightening or a cause for anxiety, showing to us parts of our character that we normally overlay with distraction. The question of place is not simply that of finding an external setting which is silent and apart, but even more important, finding within ourselves peace and solitude as the interior space where we pray to God. As we shall see, it is the acceptance and development of this interior peace and solitude which is the key to all growth in the spiritual life. And, once again, there is a cost to be paid, an inner crucifixion of fear and anxiety in order to discover the place of stillness within where God is.

And thirdly, there is the element of materials — how shall we pray. Having found the time and the place, we are now ready to begin to pray. But we shall need words to express ourselves, and they should be spoken with sincerity and conviction. The first requirement is a small book — preferably with loose leaves — and a pencil. In it we can put basic daily/weekly outlines of thanksgiving and intercession such as we have already considered. Then, we write in any prayers which we find helpful. These can come from many sources — prayer books, manuals of devotion, anthologies of prayer, prayer cards, etc. — and should be adapted if necessary to meet special needs. Also, we should try to pray in our own words, and sometimes a phrase or aspiration will prove just right, and find its place in our notebook. It is worth remembering that the pencil can be used to cross out what is no longer required as well as to add new things that are needed.

To help them begin to pray, many people find reading a passage from Scripture or a spiritual book helpful. The Psalms, hymn books, collects and other liturgical material can be pressed into service. A crucifix, holy pictures and other visual helps such as candles all help to focus the attention upon prayer. Making the sign of the cross can mark the beginning and end of the time given to God. Above all, the recitation of the Lord's Prayer, slowly, thoughtfully, carefully, can bring our prayer to a close with the assurance of praying according to the mind of Christ. If possible, it is helpful at this early stage to build up a portable prayer kit that is flexible in use, and can be adjusted to meet changing circumstances.

But all of these are less than useless without the recognition that the words we speak come from the silence within and enter the silence of God. We reach out to him from the solitude of our hearts and he reaches through to us from the serenity of his Godhead. Therefore, all our words, and the thoughts behind them, are best spoken slowly and quietly. Ecclesiastes reminds us that our words should be few lest we presume too much. So we avoid gabbling and chatter, being willing to allow our few words to ebb away into silence when we have nothing more to say. There will often be times when we cannot find words to express what is in our hearts. Very well, let there be silence. God reaches our hearts just the same, and, indeed, because all words are only approximations pointing to the reality they seek to express, silent worship on such occasions can reflect more accurately what we wish to communicate, than forced phrases which distort the true meaning held within the silence.

Such moments may be experienced by us as dryness, blankness, distraction, frustration or a host of other painful and potentially destructive sentiments — there is little pleasure in them for us — but we should never confuse our reactions in the conscious mind with our intentions of the heart. We want to pray; we have given the time to God; we are trying to give him our undivided attention. For God, this is enough. For him, our intention to pray and the dedication of the time is to pray, provided we hold fast in the silence, with all its undesirable effects, until the completion of the time promised. This is why it is important to experience these moments of emptiness, of the failure of words and images, before we extend our time commitment beyond the minimum.

Of course, there are distractions from without, but these are not the same. They may be caused by rushing into the time of prayer without first creating the still space of prayer within us, or through periods of anxiety derived from the pressures of daily life, or because of personal unhappiness or distress. To tackle these, we need common sense and will power to quieten the discordant noises until they form at least a background static, or preferably die away through the crystallizing of the mind upon God in carefully wrought prayer.

But the internal breaking down of words and images into dumb silence through our inability to speak is not the misfortune we might fear. True, it is painful. The cross is penetrating further into our spiritual life and breaking down the language of devotion which we have constructed, and which we have found of so much value in articulating our faith in God and commitment to Christ. However, what appears as loss of words is better seen as a gain in silence, and as we grow used to that silence, then we shall find it revealing of God in a way beyond our comprehension. Being detached from words and attached to silence is the next step in our progress towards union, which we need to explore in more detail later.

But before we do this, there is a parallel activity to prayer which should engage the mind of the convert, and it is to this we now turn.

SEVEN

True Reason

We considered in the previous chapter the first stages in the development of a prayerful life, looking at the way of praying commonly called mental prayer, that is, prayer based on thought, expressed in words, originating in images of God that convey in intellectual terms the new faith of the convert. These images of the mind, sustained in the Christian tradition by a common language of faith and found foremost in the biblical record, ensure that the new believer is introduced to the revelation of God that he has made through the ages and brought to final focus in the person of Jesus Christ. These images nourish him with spiritual truths that feed his mind with new insights into the self-disclosure that God has revealed to us in the process of bringing redemption to mankind. In this way, his intellectual faculties are given the necessary material to recast the meaning of existence around what God has revealed as true about himself and his creation. This formation of the Christian mind is essential, if the believer is to reorder the whole of his being in the service of God. The education of the convert is the concern of this chapter, so that prayer and ethics flow from an informed surrender to the will of God and not blind obedience to an impersonal set of rules.

This Christian education is partly undertaken by means of the various teaching opportunities presented by the Church — through sermons, study groups, spiritual discussions with other Christians, individual conversations with the clergy. All these channels should be explored and used as energetically as possible. Also there are spiritual books, the writings of Christians of proven worth and insight whose grasp of the life of faith has benefited the Church at large. A Christian should seek advice on suitable reading and always have a Christian book in hand, to assist this process of reforming the mind into that of Christ. For most of us, this sort of reading is as essential to our Christian life as the car manual is to the motor mechanic or the authoritative reference book to the serious student. Both contain practical treasure to be mined and applied, to remind us what is worthwhile rediscovering from the past and worth learning for the first time from what is new.

Of course, our basic Christian manual is the Bible, and the regular reading of the Scriptures is essential to the believer, if his spiritual reading as a whole is to relate to the prophetic witness to Christ contained in the Old Testament and the apostolic witness to Christ proclaimed to us in the New Testament. To claim to be a Christian without a deep working knowledge of the Bible is to open our faith to influences which have not the sanction and blessing of the Church, and which can lead us into rash assertions that we understand what it means to be a Christian, while allowing all sorts of other influences from outside the Christian tradition to fill the gap in our understanding with their partial truths or even false nonsense.

This is a particular issue for those who claim entry to the Christian faith through non-Christian techniques of meditation, or who are encouraged to seek forms of prayer beyond the use of words before they have developed the necessary understanding that produces the Christian mind, capable of grasping the meaning of the revelation God has achieved in Christ. This is a serious matter for concern that must be examined in more detail in the next chapter.

Of course, reading the Bible by itself does not necessarily make its meaning clear; nor does simply reading it protect us from misinterpretation and error. It is a book to be read from within the tradition of the Church, written as it was from faith to faith. In it, men and women of faith communicate to us who have faith, and they ask us to interpret what we read from the point of view of the faith which they held, and to which we seek to be the heirs. Therefore, it is essential that we read the Scriptures with help from commentaries and expositions by other Christians, so that we read from within a consensus of belief. If differences of interpretation occur between commentaries, then we shall need to use our present discernment to try to see the common ground and whether the matter can be resolved — if not, then appeal to a third party is legitimate. Such assistance should help us in going back into the thought processes and assumptions of the original writers, and then bring forward the meaning of their writing into contemporary significance. The issue is always what they reveal to us of the nature and activity of God and how that revelation affects our lives today.

This developed understanding of the Bible, together with all the other aspects of our intellectual development as a Christian, is not achieved in a day, but remains the task of a lifetime. Over years, it does bring about profound changes in the soul that bear fruit in our daily discipleship, provided that what we learn does not remain an intellectual achievement only. The Orthodox have a saying that we consume doctrine just as we consume the elements of the Eucharist, and this should be our aim.

In other words, such an educational programme needs to be 'earthed' to practice, and before we can do this 'earthing', the link has to be established between our understanding and our will. The mind must not be permitted to engage in mental exercises that satisfy intellectually, but are not applied to daily life. Charles Gore used to say that every clause of the creeds has both an intellectual meaning and a moral consequence. For example, we cannot affirm our faith in Jesus Christ as 'conceived by the power of the Holy Spirit and born of the Virgin Mary' while denying the dignity and value of every human being in God's eyes, and we cannot believe in one Church without working for Christian unity and practising love of the brethren.

We make this link by pondering the truths we have been studying intellectually in such a way that we focus on the personal application to which we should put them. This process of 'internalizing' the teaching of the Church in Scripture and tradition is called meditation, and this is the means by which we develop the Christian mind which instinctively thinks, feels and acts theologically, applying naturally and intuitively the faith to every area of life. In short, Christian meditation is the natural exercise of our minds upon the task of understanding and applying the truths of the Christian religion. It is not prayer as such, but an invaluable adjunct to prayer because it disposes the heart and mind towards the things of God and gives us a context within which to pray with understanding.

But to describe Christian meditation thus immediately raises the issue of meditation in other contexts. It clearly is very similar to the sort of meditation on a problem, done by a person at work. For example, an engineer will consider carefully what he knows to be true about various aspects of his area of expertise, and then apply those considerations to the issue at hand. But not all uses of the word 'meditation' are like this.

So-called scientific transcendental meditation claims to have no basis in religious faith (although its roots are clearly in eastern religion), but its approach is anything but scientific. Rather, its aim is to eliminate particular knowledge by suspending the usual mental processes which we call thinking. And to do this, the practitioner is required to repeat a meaningless sound until he enters a trance-like state of relaxation closely akin to being asleep. Indeed, scientific research on this type of meditation indicates that the effects produced are indistinguishable from our usual sleep patterns. This is not the way to proceed if we seek to understand and apply the truths of religion to the life of faith.

The openly religious form of meditation practised by Hinduism and Buddhism is also intended to achieve something far different from Christian meditation. Its goal is to produce a sense of nothingness, an absence of all things and everything, so that the soul is put in touch with the impersonal abyss of divinity that is the goal of Hinduism, which abyss Buddha believed to be literally nothing, because for him divinity does not exist and is not even beyond existence. To be brought into such an abyss is in Hindu thought to lose all sense of self within the impersonal deity, and in Buddhist thought to be totally extinguished and cease to be, even in an impersonal form.

To achieve this, Hindu and Buddhist meditation requires the denial of individual desiring, the loss of personal self, the rejection of conscious separation from other things. And the technique is, once again, the inculcation of a trance-like state by the recitation of a mantra, a meaningless sound, to hypnotize and suppress all that the Christian understanding of man believes is central to his relationship with God — the maintenance of identity, person, will, conscious and desired attachment in love. Some of the language may be the same in the different religions, but the words mean different things. For the Hindu and the Buddhist, their goal is a union with Godhead in which all that constitutes the individual self is absorbed or lost into an impersonal abyss of divinity, a divinity which for the Buddha, though not for all his followers, is seen as non-existent, so that death to self in a union with divinity becomes total destruction of even the impersonal, absorbed existence that Hinduism affirms.

Such an understanding of union with God is totally opposed to the Christian revelation, with its commitment by a personal God to a promise of union with him for all believers, a union in which the personal is enhanced, not lost, all desiring is fulfilled, not denied, and consciousness remains individual, within a community of love in which the personal God whom we worship is eternally the focus of our delight and our joy. For us, personal relationship not only remains in our union with God — it is reordered, enhanced and perfected. And to the extent that we begin this process in this life we discover that we have eternal life now.

To do this, our programme of instruction needs to be meditative in character. Hopefully, we shall read the Bible regularly, preferably daily, and take the same precautions as with mental prayer to achieve the time, place and materials for the task, making similar provision as well for the other aspects of our intellectual input. But, the understanding gained becomes spiritually beneficial, only when the material is pondered upon deeply, carefully, and digested, producing practical results in the life of faith.

There are many methods of meditation, with varying degrees of intellectual content, depending on the personality and background of the person using them. One method may find itself more easily used by a person of academic training, used to working with ideas; another may suit a person little interested in abstract concepts but with a good imagination.

One method which is very adaptable and can be used profitably by a wide range of people is known as the 'five-p' method, so named after the five steps of the meditation — prepare, picture, ponder, pray, promise.

An example of how this works out in practice is as follows.

Consider the healing of the leper in St Mark 1, 40–45.

Prepare   Read the passage slowly and attentively. Ask for the guidance of the Holy Spirit to direct your thoughts. Then, read through two or three times, noting various points raised by the text. For example, note the strong emphasis on the emotions of Jesus — moved with pity; he sternly charged him — the humanity of Jesus is affirmed; also the faith of the leper and his appeal to the will of Christ to do good; the response of Jesus, 'I will', and the authoritative command, 'Be clean' — the voice of God, the desire of Jesus to fulfil the law of Moses regarding leprosy. But the leper ignores Jesus' command. Why? Also Jesus shows his pity in a practical way by touching the leper, thereby breaking a taboo that lepers were 'untouchable'. For the leper healing brings release from alienation and return to society — it is his redemption from oppression. He becomes an evangelist for Jesus, but creates difficulties for him by raising his popularity. Why did Jesus wish his work to be secret? What false hopes did Jesus wish to avoid in the population?

Picture   Using the imagination, build up a mental picture of the event. Jesus is walking along a dusty road in the open countryside. A town is nearby. The sky is blue; it is hot and sunny; alongside the road are fields and vineyards and orchards; his disciples are with him and they are talking to him and to each other about the extraordinary happenings of the last few days. Then a figure comes out of the field, and approaches them. He is disfigured and crippled by leprosy — an outcast of society, feared and yet pitied because of the disease. He speaks to Jesus directly, believing that Jesus can heal him if only he is willing to do so. Jesus expresses his pity directly and effectively by touching the man — the disciples are horrified by this reckless act — and holding him firmly declares that he is willing to help. The healing takes place at once. Then Jesus' tone of voice becomes stern and he orders the man to keep his healing a secret between him and them. He must make the offering that the law requires because he is known as a leper, but the source of his cure must not be told. The leper, now healed, leaves Jesus and cannot contain the joy within himself and begins to tell others how he was healed. This miracle causes a sensation and turns Jesus into a local celebrity. One act of pity has turned into a media event.

Ponder   Where am I in the story?

Am I the leper? Where in my life do I need to be healed — emotionally, physically, intellectually, spiritually? How much do I in fact recognize my dependence on the will of God for my good?

Am I Jesus? As a member of his Body, do I touch the lives of others, especially those who are untouchable, with a pity that achieves practical good? How important is it to affirm the humanity of others by touching them at every level of their being? How frightened am I of convention, or of the involvement to which such touching may well lead? How do I distinguish between improper touching for my own self-satisfaction and the touch that heals?

Am I one of the disciples? What do I learn about Jesus as God and Jesus as man in this incident? How do I cope with elements of unbelief in my life that cause Jesus to be a scandal to me?

Am I one of the crowds who are attracted to Jesus? Do I run to him to look for a cure, for success, for selfish motives? Or do I see him as the God who is moved to pity towards me, and whom in return I seek because I want to give my life to him?

How does St Mark show Jesus as human? What do I learn from him about being human? What does he teach me in this miracle about the nature of God? How should I respond to that revelation?

Pray Now bring the fruits of pondering into the form of prayer, thanking God for all that has been shown of his purposes in Jesus, and asking him to guide you to respond appropriately that day to the message of the miracle.

Promise Take just *one* thing from the event and make a promise to try to put it into effect. Make the promise specific and straightforward, e.g. I will show more pity towards Mary in the office today and listen to her problems; I will take care not to sensationalize my relationship with Jesus when I talk about it; I will not differentiate between people by trusting those I like and not trusting those I dislike; I will avoid back-slapping bonhomie that degrades physical contact by its falsity, especially with colleagues at work.

This method of meditation can be applied flexibly to accommodate most types of people. Those with little imagination will shorten the picture; those with little intellectual ability will shorten the preparation; those with well developed intuition will move quickly from pondering into prayer, but all should give attention to the promise because this is the test of the value of the meditation, that what has been prepared, pictured, pondered and prayed over bears fruit in our life.

Sometimes the promise may be repeated over several days or weeks because it contains a lesson we find hard to learn. Sometimes the season of the year provides a theme for several weeks of meditation, e.g. Christmas and Epiphany, Holy Week and Easter. When the text for our meditation is not from the Gospel, e.g. St Paul's letters, the element of picturing is not always necessary. At all times a simple book of theological words and ideas is a helpful reference source for the initial preparation when we read over the text.

Of course, some people find reading is not very useful and much prefer a practical means of meditating. Here the rosary can come into its own, providing the believer with a mystery to be pictured and pondered, prayers to be said, and the beads passing through the fingers as an aid to maintaining attention. Although the rosary is, in its traditional form, associated with the repetition of the *Ave Maria*, there is no reason why other set prayers such as the *Gloria Patri* or *Kyrie* should not be used instead. The rosary has been the mainstay of building the Christian mind for the majority of Christians over many centuries, and its themes of the incarnation, passion and crucifixion, resurrection and glorification of our Lord have retained the central mysteries of the faith in the daily consciousness of its users in a way that can hardly be bettered.

Another more practical form of meditation is to read a passage from the Gospels and then apply the action or teaching of Jesus directly to our life through reference to our feet, hands and lips. Where is the Lord asking me to take my feet today? What is the Lord calling me to do with my hands today? What does the Lord require me to speak with my lips today? In this simple way, we assimilate into our lives the dispositions, actions and thoughts of Jesus and conform ourselves more and more to his example. The Gospel events are translated across into our lives, and in doing so, the attitudes and vices that deny Christ are driven out. In this form of meditation, the person needs a good imagination to make the link between himself and Jesus, and an intuitive grasp of the point the evangelist is making in the event described. Such a method can prove invaluable for a person of little formal education who is more at home in the realm of picture language than that of abstract ideas.

Applying this method to the healing of the leper already considered, we may realize that Jesus is asking us to walk towards those in distress or need, to reach out to them with our hands to assure them of our compassion and concern, and to speak to them of God's presence in our lives, assuring them that he is willing them to turn to him for help, healing and the discovery that he cares for them.

This educational process, which is made fruitful by meditation, provides the context within which our mental prayer grows, and therefore meditation should find a secure place in our reordered life. Daily meditation for, say, ten minutes before the commencement of prayer is ideal, but, if this cannot be managed, a regular routine such as three times a week, or for an hour over the weekend must be our objective, if we wish to take our new faith seriously. A believer who does not meditate must soon expect his prayers to become stale, as there is no spring of inspiration from which to refresh his soul and renew his will in its purpose. Thanksgiving becomes routine and then, tragically devalued, it ceases for lack of impetus. And, once this happens, mental prayer is reduced to a treadmill of repentance without real discipleship and intercession without a living sense of God's will.

But if meditation is made upon our intellectual input to educate and produce the Christian mind, then all the strengths of the soul are galvanized into action and harnessed to the practice of prayer and the reformation of character.

These include the satisfaction of the senses with spiritual delights, so that we find pleasure in worship and prayer, the sacraments, spending time in meditation, making progress in virtue and sharing our life with fellow Christians. This sensual satisfaction is usually effective in detaching us from our past, and leads to emotional gains in all these areas as well. We feel good and enjoy our religion. Life has purpose and we sense that we are being guided by God's grace towards holiness.

Coupled with this delight in the senses towards religion goes the recasting of our powers of imagination

in the service of Christ. Our pondering during meditation helps our imagination to see the hand of God in the
ordinary events of daily life. This, coupled with the
power of intuition, is enormously helpful in moving us
quickly from earth-bound considerations to the joys of a
life lived with Christ and for Christ.

All these aspects of the soul, its senses, imagination,
intuition, and emotion, together give us an enhanced
experience of being alive, and on the basis of the
pleasure they bring us we find our intellectual life
becomes conformed also to the quest for union with
God.

The understanding grows in appreciation of the riches
of faith, so that its meaning is deepened and enlarged to
embrace the whole of the purpose of life — belief
becomes the guiding light of understanding, and practical trust in God's good providence undergirds daily
living. The memory becomes filled with the remembrance of God's graciousness towards us, as the benefits
of increased understanding are stored up and later recalled to inspire us in our discipleship. On the basis of
remembered blessings received, hope is born in the soul
and takes wings as we look forward to an even greater
sharing in the life of Christ, with its culmination in
union with God. The will, strengthened and guided by
faith in the understanding and hope in the memory, is
drawn to the virtue of love, and seeks to practise ever
more closely the imitation of Christ's love, until all of
life is consumed in a willed offering of ourselves to the
way of the cross.

These three fundamental Christian virtues of faith,
hope and love, actively developing in the understanding, memory and will, through co-operation with the
will of God, are the fruit of progressively conforming
our lives at every level from the physical through to the
intellectual to the call of Jesus to follow him. What
started as a break with the past life, lived in sin and

unbelief, has become a reordered and dedicated life, surrendered to the service of Christ and to seeking union with God. We have actively sought this change by working with the grace of God. We have used our natural powers to the best of our ability. These have brought us as far as they can take us. Now the time of active co-operation is drawing to a close and God takes the initiative once again, only this time we have nothing more to offer and the change wrought in us comes entirely from God. We find ourselves passive, unable to act, but his grace moves us on into unknown and strange territory, where the spiritual life must be lived in a new manner. The way forward remains that of the cross, but the cross is experienced so differently from what has gone before that many now fall by the wayside. Therefore, we must now consider this passive stage in our spiritual progress.

EIGHT

Growing Pains

We have now reached the point where the convert is in a settled habit of Christian discipleship defined by mental prayer, meditation, the sacramental life, reformation of character and good works.

These last three will continue to provide him for the rest of his life with a call to obedience which will maintain his following of Christ in a deepening, renewing pattern that will lead him towards holiness. No doubt there will be setbacks as well as progress. Repentance and forgiveness remain the rhythm of advance for us. At times, the grace of God will reveal new areas of sacrifice where virtues practised will need to be applied to aspects of our life which we had previously thought already conformed to Christ. Also, what is held to be a moral duty should become increasingly an instinctive loving response, so that what the will began as a self-denying ordinance is transformed steadily into a chosen expression of our true heart's desire. Supporting and sustaining all this is a regular sacramental life, formed out of a God-centred sense of priorities that ensures time and opportunity are found for regular, frequent sharing in the Eucharist. These three continuing expressions of a committed faith remain necessary to our integrity before God, and provide us with the context within which developments in the practice of prayer occur. It is with these developments that the rest of this book is concerned.

The effect of mental prayer and meditation is two-fold. First, mental prayer causes us to direct our minds towards God, and the parts of prayer lead us to see how the whole of our existence can be brought into relationship with grace. Faith expresses its central dedication to God in daily praying that articulates how God has become the centre of our life. Secondly, meditation, together with mental prayer, reorders our understanding of existence in terms of the revealed nature of God and his graciousness towards us. The Christian mind is formed around divine revelation, harnessing our intellectual abilities to the service of Christ and to the pursuit of a philosophy of life arising out of faith.

But revelation is a divine activity, designed to illuminate our understanding, so that faith is supported by reason. As such, its task is to communicate with mankind what is needed to make faith possible. Revelation makes the difference between religion and philosophy. However, once faith is planted in the soul, then the purpose of revelation becomes seen as a vital but limited necessity. It is vital, because it sets out in terms we can understand what God is like; it is limited, because the likeness of God is shown to us in intellectual terms, and intellectual terms always distort to some extent the truth they seek to convey.

To put this another way, every time we use a word to communicate with another we are forming an idea in the mind. Language is the sharing of ideas. Every time we form a sentence we are setting out a series of ideas. Applying this to meditation, to think about God is to make a series of models or images of God in our minds that help us to understand him. Equally, mental prayer offers to God a string of concepts that together give verbal expression to our faith. But faith is not contained by the concepts used; rather the concepts are themselves a series of intellectual approximations to a faith which is better seen as a living relationship than as an intellectual encounter. The living God in whom we have faith is more than the intellectual categories in which he is described. Revelation produces a set of models which act as pointers to the nature of God beyond the intellectual. God is neither the product of our minds, nor of our emotions, nor of any aspect of our nature, but rather he uses these things to share with us a divine flow of ideas that together provide us with guidance in the right direction, away from wrong images and towards his true self which lies beyond images.

Words are good, but not good enough. Images are necessary at first, but not sufficient to bring us to union with the true God. The purpose of language is to hold the ring within which the search for God takes place; or, perhaps better, the understanding needs to be satisfied intellectually before we can safely move on beyond understanding in our progress towards union.

Thus the Athanasian Creed describes God as incomprehensible, which means that we cannot grasp God as a concept or a feeling — he is not the product of our intellect or emotions — but rather it is God who grasps us to himself in the mystery of faith. He embraces us and we discover ourselves caught up into his love, the reality of which convicts us even though we cannot adequately describe what he has done to us. God remains a mystery to us because he is beyond us and yet with us.

So it is that, for the person of faith, the mystery of God is not a scientific puzzle to be solved by reason, but a compelling truth which we cannot deny without losing the ultimate meaning of human life. For us, the incomprehensible nature of God both saves us from idolatry, the worship of powerful images by the intellect and good sensations in the emotions, and teaches us that humility must apply to the mind and heart in our search for union with God, because neither can carry us all the way into the presence of the mystery which is the Holy Trinity. He is our goal; he leads us along the right paths; he takes each and every aspect of our human nature and brings into perfect alignment with his will; thus he requires us to move on beyond their resources, relying in faith alone upon his grace to bring us to himself.

What we are seeking, as our first objective, is a gathering up of our human powers, the strengths of our soul, to the point where they find their own fulfilment in a satisfaction which comes from spiritual pleasures. Then we move forward in faith beyond these spiritual pleasures into a yet closer relationship with God. Thus, mental prayer and meditation feast the intellect with revealed spiritual truths that excite and satisfy the understanding; the memory finds great delight in recalling those pleasures so that the remembrance of worldly pleasures ceases to compare; the emotions are fulfilled with the spiritual feelings that come from prayer, worship and the sacraments; and the will is happily reordered towards satisfaction in the will of God, because love for God becomes our delight and our purpose for living. But this is not the end of our journey. God asks yet more of us than the reordering of our souls upon spiritual satisfactions.

At this point, God acts decisively in the soul to require us to surrender our need for pleasure. He asks us to forgo the spiritual satisfaction that means so much to us and to move forward from loving him for our own sakes to loving him for his own sake. These pleasures, because they rely upon the active exercise of our human strengths, cannot bring us into union with the incomprehensible God. And this is not because these pleasures are wrong, but because they are limited in their scope and in their power. Their scope is determined by our ability to make images, to generate feelings, to recall past satisfactions; their power is no more than that of our souls at full stretch.

Humanly speaking, we have done all we can to grow

towards God; now he must carry us forward entirely by his grace and we must rest passively in his hands. He has grasped us in his love, and he now draws us away from all that we have relied upon so far in the spiritual life so that his grace really becomes sufficient for us. This is a moment of great risk and a time of intense suffering. Once again we are being refined in the fire of God's love by being asked to take up the cross of Christ and walk forward with him in faithful obedience to the promptings of the Holy Spirit.

What happens is this. Mental prayer begins to prove difficult. As we pray, we find that the words and phrases that used to mean so much to us appear to lose their meaning. What was illuminating and helpful becomes boring, useless, empty. The intellect ceases to take any pleasure or to gain satisfaction from praying, because we find it hard to form any meaningful words with which to pray. The old patterns collapse and we cannot muster our mental forces to shape up new patterns to take their place. Our prayer runs into the sand and we are faced with a dark void in the understanding.

At the same time, meditation fails. Those long-loved methods of stirring up the understanding and the feelings to work together and produce spiritual delights in the mind and heart seem now to be useless. They cease to teach us those divine truths which we had enjoyed savouring intellectually and emotionally, and applying to our lives. We try to meditate, but find it impossible. Our understanding fails; our imagination is unable to give support; our memory of previous meditation experience is found to be irrelevant; we flounder in mental darkness and find it intensified by the loss of good feelings which until now have accompanied our growth in spiritual understanding. All that has been gained in spiritual growth seems in jeopardy.

The temptation at this point is to unbelief. It seems

that what promised so much at the start of the venture of faith has failed to bring lasting benefits to us. Our faculties have been drawn along a path which now peters out, leaving us stranded, disappointed, even angry and despairing. We appear to have been the victims of a confidence trick, more demonic than divine, and we look fools to ourselves and will soon be seen as such by others to whom we have spoken so eloquently of the Christian life.

But if this is how we feel then it is our pride that is hurt, and in particular our intellectual pride. We need to recall the limitations of our understanding in the life of faith and the servant role which it plays in the purposes of God. Its true task is to lead us to this point of darkness, not to presume that it can overcome the darkness ahead through more strenuous intellectualizing and more deft juggling of ideas. The understanding is now being blinded by the grace of God in order that we should both recognize its limitations and begin to detach ourselves from dependence upon it. This is the time for the humbling of intellectual pride before the mystery of the Holy Trinity, whose incomprehensible nature breaks down all image-making by our intellect. We are being purged by the experience of dereliction so that we do not cling to them as a substitute for God. Union with spiritual pleasures, good as they are, is not union with God, and to find ourselves stripped of them is to be seen as an expression of confidence in us on God's part that we are ready to proceed under his guidance beyond reliance upon spiritual pleasures into the darkness of his incomprehensible being. The suffering we undergo is sent to us for our good and is required, if we are to follow in the steps of Christ on the way of the cross. Devoid of human support, divested of even good sensations, we move forward naked, to seek to be clothed with a new robe at the hands of the one who loves us so much, that he allows us to suffer in order to reward us further with a deeper union than that already attained.

For each of us the onset of this new phase in our prayer takes a particular form, reflecting the differing strengths of the individual soul. No one person experiences this stripping of spiritual pleasures in exactly the same way or to the same extent as another. Crucifixion of the senses comes to all who tread the way of the cross, but the manner of its coming, the length it takes and its effects upon the soul differ widely. However, by describing two common patterns of experience, we may be able to recognize ourselves and our own loss of meditation and mental prayer.

Some people have the sort of personality which holds thought and feeling apart. The intellect and the emotions are not integrated but operate to a large extent independently of each other. For such a person, conversion tends to occur, first of all, either in the area of understanding or in the area of feelings. Where the person is intellectually gifted, if conversion is primarily an emotional matter, then the temptation is to divorce faith from understanding right from the beginning, so that faith rapidly turns intellectually philistine and the formation of the Christian mind becomes stilted by infantile dogmatism. Such a person hardly ever penetrates the mysteries of faith because God becomes for him a series of emotional satisfactions justified by narrow opinions. If, however, the living God does break through these intellectual defences by the use of doubt or emotional distress, then the pain that follows is severe and the need for support vital to the survival of faith in that person. What is more, that support will need to come from outside the circle of like-minded persons in which such a Christian tends to move.

If, on the other hand, the conversion is primarily in the intellect, then an intellectually gifted person whose thoughts and feelings are usually kept apart will find that the life of faith follows a different path. Here intellectual exploration and satisfaction leads to great advances in the practice of meditation, and the application of its fruits produces a systematic reordering of the will around obedience to the will of God. It may be that mental prayer is fairly dry, predictable, even dull, but it is practised dutifully, because we are commanded to do so. The same applies to the sacramental life. Faith settles on good works, informed with growing understanding. The emotions may be rarely engaged, if at all, to assist the will and are perhaps seen even as a hindrance. Held in check, they lie unharnessed and their strengths untapped. The soul develops intellectually to the point of maturity but feelings and imagination are left behind. They may not be needed very much even for meditation, but neither are they to hand with adequate compensations when the intellect begins to fail under the impact of God's blinding grace. For such a person, the deprivation that comes from the loss of power to meditate is more devastating than the inability to practise mental prayer. The mind reels in confusion, floundering in the darkness. No matter how much effort and application is made, the results are chaotic. Reliable signposts disappear, familiar trains of thought become meaningless, attempts to recast old ideas into new forms just cannot be done. Faith hangs unsupported, inarticulate, lifeless, and the will to believe starts to falter. Prayer, once dry perhaps, now becomes an agony and worship pointless. All seems lost, and our feelings, so long held at arm's length by the intellect, have their revenge, by reinforcing its blindness with their own sense of deprivation and suffering. For such people, this moment in the spiritual life is like a fracture. A bone snaps within and pain sears through them.

For those whose intellect and emotions interact freely, so that intellectual exercises are pursued with the support of feelings, a quite opposite set of experiences is likely. Conversion, in these circumstances, galvanizes thoughts and feelings to work together in the reordering of the soul upon the Christian life. Whether the intellect is gifted or weak, the emotions are galvanized to assist in meditation, to reinforce the practice of mental prayer and to find pleasure in worship and in good works. Working hand in glove, the intellect and the emotions often progress rapidly and the satisfaction found fuels development. The temptation to enthusiasm may sometimes lead to spiritual exhaustion, but rarely to a major crisis. The concern in the early days is more often that of maintaining steady control rather than that of needing encouragement. But once the convert recognizes his limitations and his immaturity in faith, then sustained development becomes possible, until the point is reached when God starts to remove the spiritual pleasures that have been the very stimulus to growth. In this case, because the practice of meditation is often focused more on imagination and practical action than on intellectual enlightenment, and because the intellect is supported constructively by the emotions, the transition into the darkness caused by loss of spiritual pleasures is usually fairly gentle. Short periods of aridity and blankness, followed by a resumption of the usual familiar pattern of devotions, gradually ease the soul from one state to the next. Indeed, for some there may never be a complete transfer, and the soul will live in both states, sometimes practising meditation of a very simple kind together with straightforward mental prayer, often reduced to small phrases and aspirations, while at other times holding itself content to be still and silent in the God-given darkness. For some, the transition is so natural that it occurs with hardly any notice. Instead of the pain of a fracture, here there is the embracing of a familiar friend, whose unexpected arrival under a new guise has taken us, perhaps, by surprise.

Most of us fall somewhere in between these two types. We neither keep our intellect and our emotions wholly apart, nor do they interact freely and happily. Rather, for the majority, our intellect and our emotions do impinge upon each other, sometimes harmoniously, sometimes destructively. Negative feelings are often especially hard to integrate with our intellect, and cause considerable dislocation in meditation and prayer and in the application of understanding to the decision-making of the will. This mixed bag of differing and often conflicting interests, which we call our personality, has a profound influence on the development of spiritual pleasures and the timing and manner of their loss.

Although God calls all to progress towards union with himself, the timing is very much in our hands at the start. Perseverance in the reordering of the powers of the soul around the will of God is critical, and setbacks may occur either because of the deep-rootedness of sin in us or because we lack the application to the task. Both can lead to serious delays. Also, serious disharmony within the soul can undermine or complicate progress, especially when this results in a weakened sense of identity or value as a person, so that our foundations are unsure. Often we need internal healing and reconciliation as the fundamental experience of salvation in order to make progress towards our destiny of union with God.

All these factors point to the need of skilled help in guiding us towards a true assessment of our spiritual state and of whether we have still further progress to make before we encounter the moment when we can do no more, or whether that moment has come and we must accept the darkness that envelops us. The dearth of knowledgeable spiritual directors remains a scandal and a cause of much distress in the Church.

But, with all the diversity of experience, there emerges enough common ground to enable us to ask four basic questions to all who may be at this critical point in their spiritual pilgrimage. These are:

Do I still want to pray?

Can I practise mental prayer?

Can I meditate?

Am I in a state of serious sin?

Obviously, the answers to the questions, and perhaps especially the last, may not be easily found, but if the basic response to the first is affirmative, and to the others negative, then it is likely that God has brought you to the point of darkness and has begun the process of stripping away spiritual pleasures in order to lead you forward to the life of faith undertaken out of love for him alone. If the answers to any one (or more) of the four questions is otherwise, then we must look within ourselves to discover why we seem to have come up against a block in our prayer. Once again, direction can be very helpful in bringing to light some of the causes that are producing the symptoms of distress which we are facing.

One last matter remains, left over from the last chapter, namely that of understanding the needs of those who move quickly into darkness through non-Christian methods of prayer and meditation, or by the immediate use of non-verbal forms of prayer at the start of their Christian life.

For the first group, the issue is at heart a confusion of language so that what is called meditation by both Christians and non-Christians is accepted as the same. In fact, as we have seen in the previous chapter, they are quite different, even opposed to each other. Behind each lies a vision of God which is radically at variance with the other, and, therefore, to leave a person in the darkness of non-Christian meditation is to give them up to a life of prayer which is out of touch with the Holy Trinity. They are on the path to a union with the divine which is not the way of Christ, and they need, for their own sakes, to be led back, or to retrace their footsteps, in order to enter by the narrow gate of Jesus that leads to salvation. What is at stake is a return to an understanding of human nature in terms of the goodness and rightness of individuality and personality, of the indispensable need to be a desiring creature in order to find God, and of the central role of the will, supported by the various intellectual and sensual strengths of the soul, in attaining to the heavenly vision. Our vision of God creates directly our vision of human nature and human potential. Doctrines of God and of man are not independent; the former creates the latter. Therefore, the person who has come to faith in Christ and yet has been using non-Christian techniques of prayer and meditation needs, first and foremost, the formation of the Christian mind in order to undo the deformation that has occurred. Meditation, in the Christian sense, and the practice of mental prayer are lifelines that inform the Christian life and prevent an esoteric mysticism that hovers between ecstasy and boredom.

If this seems harsh, then we need to remember that all of us are deformed by the current philosophy of the age, by insidious agnosticism and relativism, by the retreat from truth into expediency, and by the refusal to act on principle if political advantage lies in the direction of popular approval for the second-rate and the indifferent. In all of us, the formation of the Christian mind is not the shaping up of faith from scratch, but the reshaping of our understanding after the pattern of Christ in the context of a life already heavily influenced by the world.

However, in the case of those who plunge into non-verbal prayer and attempt contemplative techniques right from the start, the issue may well be simply that of gentle adjustment. Accepting that we all need to discover the mind of Christ and to recognize that the influences of the world have to be faced and reversed, at least the vision of God sought is a Christian one, and this will help the convert in this position to move naturally towards the reading of Scripture and to seek the teaching ministry of the Church in the development of his understanding. It may turn out that the greatest dangers are boredom and pride. The boredom is that of a mind underfed with Christian truth, roaming around restless and unsatisfied. The pride comes from the foolishness that is pleased with early successes in contemplation, refuses to face the inadequacy of its understanding of the Christian way, and looks down upon mental prayer as inferior. The truth is that the convert in this position is hardly weaned, let alone capable of solid food, and must humbly seek a mixture of stillness and activity, silence and mental prayer, especially penitence and intercession, to give depth and a balance to the heady but shallow experiences of adoration and 'out-of-self' moments that have been his diet so far. Also, it must be added, that the test of prayer is the fruit it produces, and a regular sacramental life, a sincere seeking to imitate Christ, and the practice of good works are clear indicators whether or not such prayer has any depth beyond self-pleasure or any influence beyond personal well-being.

NINE

Travelling by Night

We are considering the point in the spiritual life, where we are at a crossroads with regards to meditation and mental prayer. Either we cling to a futile attempt to stir up spiritual pleasures within the soul as the stimulus to prayer and devotion, or we accept that God is taking these pleasures away and plunging us into darkness and confusion, probably accompanied by pain and anguish in the soul.

But, it may be argued, such darkness is not what we deserve — we have sweated long and hard and our discipleship ought to be rewarded with something better; or that darkness is not the appropriate next step — surely spiritual pleasures should be followed by the pleasure of possessing God himself. The degree of attractiveness in these arguments is in proportion to the immaturity of our faith. They emerge from a self-centredness that thinks it knows what is possible and what is best. If we wish to construct the divine in an image of our own devising then we can have what we want, though the irony about idolatory is that it gives us not only what we want but also what we would prefer to deny we want — our sin set up as our god.

The great writers on the spiritual life present us with three reasons why God chooses to lead us on from meditation and mental prayer into a collapse of our abilities which we experience as darkness. First, the development of spiritual pleasures has given us the incentive and the compensation we need to make a concerted effort to root out the sin in our lives and to seek to replace it with virtue. We have enjoyed our life in Christ because the intellect has been fed with the truths of the Gospel; the emotions have been engaged in worship and spiritual exercises; the recalling to mind in the memory of past spiritual pleasures has both encouraged us to look forward to more of the same and given us support in resisting temptations to sin; and the will has found through spiritual pleasures unforeseen power to reorder our life after the pattern of Christ. Any deprivation due to loss of sinful pleasures has been more than adequately rewarded with spiritual gains, and the pleasure principle itself has been harnessed to galvanize the strengths of the soul to the pursuit of holiness. Now God takes away our spiritual pleasures while expecting us to maintain the progress we have made away from the pleasures of sin. Our compensations are gone and we feel deprived. We are to hold to what we have gained, not because we enjoy a tangible spiritual benefit, but because it is God's will that we do so. The emotions are stilled and put to sleep as props for the practice of virtue and the rejection of sin, and a thick blanket falls across them, which renders them heedless of our cries for help.

Secondly, the nature of faith requires darkness to be the appropriate context for the next stage in our journey to union with God. Our understanding is illuminated by knowledge and enjoys acquiring it. But the knowledge which the understanding seeks is scientific knowledge, that is to say, 'knowing about' things. The understanding collects information, factual data, and puts them together logically to produce constructions of thought, theories, models, images, which help us to dissect and reconstitute our environment, to increase our grip on the world around us and to improve on the benefits we can gain from this. As such, the understanding is not relating directly to the context of our existence, including God as the creator of all things, and tends to place us over against our context by seeking to be objective. So it is that theology, scientific knowledge about God, derived from reason and revelation, is concerned with constructing systems of faith, models and images of God, in an attempt to explain and expound the way God acts in his world. But in the end, theology must be more concerned with the breaking of images than their making, and any statement of theology is at least provisional and certainly inadequate. The understanding points us in the right direction towards where God is, but cannot carry us all the way into the heart of the mystery. 'Knowing about' has to surrender to 'knowing', the objective attempt falters in the face of the incomprehensible and we move forward in faith, unsupported by understanding, into the darkness of belief and trust. In fact this darkness which blinds the understanding, so that we walk by faith alone, is not unknown in other spheres of life. A couple may know a great deal about each other and even know each other in an intuitive way, but the commitment to marriage is still an act of faith, unsupported by conclusive evidence of a scientific kind that it will succeed. Indeed, all friendship and intimacy is based on trust, beyond what can be guaranteed by reason. To become vulnerable to another is always a step in the dark, a leap of faith, in which we sometimes suffer, or perhaps in which we are prepared for suffering because we believe the decision to be the right one. To try to live without faith in others is to seek the security that only death can provide. The analogy applies directly to our relationship with God. There is no certainty derived from the understanding, only the enigmatic assurance of faith that all will be well if we but launch out from the shallows of spiritual pleasure into the dark deep of God's love — or rather, God himself sweeps us out from the shallows into the deep and calls upon us to walk on the waters of faith instead of planting our feet on the beach of spiritual pleasure.

And thirdly, the very object of our journey himself requires that we proceed by way of darkness. His nature is incomprehensible to the intellect. He is beyond the power of reason to fathom and explain. His being is larger than what can be reached by the emotions. Their embrace cannot gather him up without remainder. We cannot put our arms around God and declare that we have him; instead he puts his arms around us and holds us to himself, saying, 'Peace, be still'. Just as a child is content to be held and suckled at the breast, so too we should be content to be held and fed by the grace of God. But to be suckled, one must suck, and to be filled with grace we must be open to receive it as it is presented to us. If darkness is God's way, then we must accept the dark in order to discover within it the means of grace offered to us. All the language we use to describe God — infinite, eternal, almighty, all-knowing, uncreated, perfect, beautiful, true, good and so on — has now run into the sand on the shore, and we are left speechless on the face of the deep in the presence of a dark glory, an undefined holiness and an ineffable love. It is to living and praying within the embrace of this obscure presence that we must now grow accustomed. And to do so, we must radically change our approach.

The common term for this darkness is 'night', from which comes that well-known phrase, 'the dark night of the soul', popularized by St John of the Cross, but badly misunderstood and misapplied in common parlance. Because we move at conversion from unbelief to faith, and from a life conditioned by sin towards the practice of virtue, there is a certain darkness in the Christian life even from the start. Deprivation, due to increasing loss of the pleasures of sin, causes darkness in the senses and the understanding from the start; faith is never intellectual certainty, even at conversion, and therefore contains from the beginning the darkness of belief and trust;

and God is as incomprehensibly other than us at the beginning as he will remain throughout our earthly pilgrimage. This means that the Christian travels by night throughout his journey, even when he is helped on his way by spiritual pleasures in the understanding and the emotions. What is happening now is that the darkness is intensifying, as a night when the clouds obscure even what little light comes from the moon and the stars. Therefore 'the dark night of the soul' is none other than the whole experience of the pilgrimage of faith experienced in deepening intensity as the journey proceeds. To equate a period of trial or suffering with 'the dark night of the soul' is to trivialize and distort the true meaning of the phrase, even though it must be said that trial or suffering can be an additional burden to a soul already stretched by the impact of God's grace upon it. But such trial or suffering is not to be seen as the moment to lapse from faith; rather, it is the opportunity to exercise faith more strenuously, remembering the cry of Christ on the cross, 'Father, into your hands I commit my spirit'.

Furthermore, this dark night has a beneficial side effect over and above its value to us as the context of the pilgrimage of faith. It also assists us in our pilgrimage away from the tyranny of the emotions and the intellect, and away from the dominance of the physical appetites. None of these things is bad in itself — to assert so would be to deny the goodness of creation — but all three can be unruly in their demands. Our sin lies in the failure of the will to resist their demands when they become aggressive, power-seeking, threatening to the balance and harmony of soul and body.

To discover the limitations of the intellect in our quest for God is to see its limitations in other areas of life and especially in the realm of human relationships. The desire of the understanding to produce conclusive evidence that it is safe to relate to another is death to all spontaneity, intuition and vulnerability. The tomb of absolute security was the dream of the Pharaohs. They did not achieve it even for their embalmed corpses, and neither shall we during our lifetime, should we try to embalm our desire for relationship in intellectual certainty. The result is cynicism and despair of finding another who will not let us down. Like Rousseau, we shall grow to love man and to hate men. All friendship relies on openness, vulnerability, and the understanding cannot speak definitively to these. To open ourselves to the darkness of God helps us to be open to the darkness of others, recognizing that we are mysterious even to ourselves and therefore the mystery at the heart of others has its attractions, even though at times it wounds as well as heals. Understanding in the intellectual sense is not all, and can never be sufficient for us at the level of the personal.

Also, our emotions, which provide the balance in intellectual dissection by being comprehensive and enveloping in their approach, are in a different way equally liable to seek to run our lives. They undermine our ability to choose and to persevere freely in the pilgrimage of faith by stirring up hopes and fears, joys and griefs, which tempt us to cling to some things and to be repelled by others. The 'dark night' shows us vividly the limitations of feelings in the quest for God and helps us to detach ourselves not only in this context but also in the context of choice in general. Our feelings are valuable as information relevant to decision-making — they should be heeded as much as the intellect and cause endless trouble if they are not — but ultimately the way we live should depend not on feelings or on intellect alone or together, but on the will of God for us, discovered in vocation, in moral decisions, in the imitation of Christ and the pursuit of virtue. Thinking and feeling the matter through takes us so far, but only waiting upon the will of God carries us to a conclusion.

Thirdly, our physical appetites, the need for the fulfilment of our desires for food and drink, our sexual desiring and our desire for 'creature comforts' are another part of our humanity which can be blessed by the 'dark night'. Too often, they are disregarded or treated as undesirable intrusions into the spiritual life, so that the unspoken assumption for many is that only the celibate and those who practise severe mortification of the flesh have any chance of real spiritual progress. Such a view is at best nonsense, and at worst, a heretical denial of our created goodness, body as well as soul. In fact, these basic human desires are both necessary to life and the very foundation of the quest for God. These essential physical desires contain the source from which all other desiring arises. Our intellectual gifts have evolved out of them. Our spiritual thirst for God exists because we know first of all what unslaked physical desire is like. We are a unity of desiring that cannot be sundered without damage to all three components, physical, intellectual and spiritual, and our emotional desires flood through all three. So it is that the Christian tradition, at its best, gives due honour and respected recognition to our physical needs. They too have the right to be harnessed and directed to the glory of God, and it is only when we deny them that right that they become unruly and rebellious. The sins which we then commit — covetousness, sloth, gluttony, lust — are more sins against our physical desires themselves than offences against God, and the guilt we incur is more a reflection of the fears and concerns of society than a sign of God's wrath. Of course, he is concerned about the abuse and misuse of what he has created good, but he knows that such behaviour springs more from pride, envy and anger in us than from the physical desires themselves.

The way in which the 'dark night' helps our physical desires is that it reinforces their intrinsic value and their positive contribution towards spiritual progress. The truth is that the sexual act does not impair or hinder our search for union with God. Instead, its place in our life is a hallowed one in which we express our sexuality physically, if called to marriage, and find that the joy and love which it brings releases us from neurosis and helps us to attend to our prayer. A happy, fulfilled sexual life is totally compatible with union with God, and if one is called to remain single, then this is not a matter of privilege or requirement in the life of prayer, but one of vocation in order to serve God in other ways. Discovering that this is true, that our prayer is unimpaired and even enhanced by the natural acceptance of our physical desires, turns them from potentially destructive denizens of the devil into delighted handmaids of the Lord.

The same is true of our desire for food and drink and 'creature comforts'. Neglected, they demand excess; recognized and honoured, they are happy to settle for a moderate, balanced and enjoyable satisfaction compatible with the claims of Christ and controlled by the 'Christian life-style'. One can be a contemplative gourmet, though perhaps not a meditative gourmand. One can enjoy beautiful things, though perhaps not be a miser or a hoarder. The truth is we need the energy that food and drink provides for spiritual as well as physical fitness, and 'creature comforts' do prevent us from dying from exposure or being tempted to the idolatry of covetousness.

We must now return to the question of how we accept the darkness of the intensified 'night' into which God has plunged us. Up till this point, we have practised meditation and mental prayer and used the spiritual pleasures resulting in the understanding and the emotions to support the will in its reformation of our life around the following of Christ. Now this ability and its resultant pleasures are gone, and we must face up to the fact that God has taken them away, because he requires us to love him more than his gifts.

Therefore, we must not try to go back to our old practices. We must not seek to meditate or attempt mental prayer. We are to let them go without regret. They have completed their task and they now belong to the past. We are not to look back, but to look forward into the impenetrable blackness of the night. Nor are we to yearn for the old spiritual pleasures that delighted us so much. They too have done their job, by bringing us to the point where they have exhausted their strengths and outlived their usefulness. We continue to receive the sacraments, imitate the life of Christ, resist temptation to sin, seek to grow in virtue, and practise a 'Christian life-style', but without the support and encouragement of spiritual satisfaction. We practise these still, because it is right to do so, and not because of what we get out of them. God is calling us to love him for his own sake, and to love his will, because in it is our peace and our good.

Instead of practising the old familiar methods of meditation and mental prayer, we are to learn a new way of praying, the way of passivity, of silence, without words. We are to rest in the darkness for our time of prayer, just willing ourselves to be there, attentive to the void that is within us and around us. God is emptying us of both our images of himself and the satisfactions that they have brought, in order to fill us with his incomprehensible self, beyond all concepts or images, and to let that incomprehensible dark presence replace our satisfactions with his unfelt but not unknown embrace.

For some, this time is one of great agony, and settling the will to be still in pain is a terrible trial. Often, the sense of helplessness is mistakenly experienced as hopelessness, but this is not the case. It is only with the passing of time that the practice of silent, willed, being in the darkness slowly becomes familiar and yields the discovery that in the darkness there is the presence of God. The pain lifts gradually as we become used to the void and we discover it strangely filled with grace and our own lives enigmatically transfigured with a dark ray of glory that heals as it pierces us through.

For many, this experience cannot be alleviated by any action on our part. God is having his way with us, and in dumb trust we surrender to his love, even though it is a love that causes us to suffer — or rather a love that exposes the limitations of our capacity to receive love and causes us pain as we grow under his guidance in order to receive it more fully. The passivity of our prayer is necessary in order that the will may be extended to receive this inflow of the divine. Much is happening on God's part, even though we are unable to co-operate actively with his grace as in the past.

However, for others, some simple aspirations in prayer are possible and helpful. In particular, the use of the name of Jesus, spoken softly, gently on the breath, or the use of the Jesus Prayer in one of its forms such as, 'Lord Jesus Christ, Son of the living God, have mercy upon us', ebbing and flowing rhythmically with our breathing, can assist us in maintaining willed being in the darkness. Such helps should be allowed to rise into the consciousness unaided, remain as long as God wills, and then freely to disappear again into the unconscious. They are never to be forced into action or retained by an act of the will — their freedom to come and go is integral to the benefit they bring to us. But, with such simple prayer, many are eased for meditation and mental prayer into a simple, loving, intuitive recognition of God's presence with them in the darkness — often called 'the prayer of loving regard', a lovely phrase that catches both the intimacy and the attention implicit in this experience of the 'dark night'.

But the form in which our darkness comes to us is in

God's hands and will be appropriate to our needs. He will present each of us with the experience necessary and helpful for the reordering of the strengths of our soul around naked faith, clinging to him in simple trust. Each of us will tread a slightly different path, even though our goal is a common one and the means of travelling will always be by night. Therefore, the passivity of the soul is doubly necessary, not only in order to discover where the Lord is leading it, but also the manner in which he is doing his gentle leading into the deeper darkness where he awaits us.

TEN

Hidden Reserves

The form of prayer in which we now find ourselves is usually called contemplation, though to describe it as the prayer of loving regard is probably a more attractive way of expressing what is happening to us. For the vast majority of Christians this is the way of prayer in which God calls them to remain for the rest of their lives. For most of us, contemplation is to become the means by which we approach the throne of grace, though to use the word 'approach' suggests more movement than is in fact required. St Augustine tells us that our approach is 'not by walking but by loving', reminding us that God is the active one in our prayer and it is our task to react to his love by loving him in return. We do not move forward to seek him, but wait lovingly in the darkness for his self-disclosure. He desires to reveal himself as present to us, but because he is who he is, we cannot, indeed dare not, expect that revelation to be any less enigmatic than was his presence with us during mental prayer, or remains Christ's presence to us in the Eucharist.

However, the fact that our God is always Emmanuel, 'God with us', encourages us to affirm that we will remain in the darkness, no matter how painful, no matter how dreary, no matter how boring, until he shows himself as with us in the way that he chooses and at the time that he chooses. Our faith is that he is with us constantly, but that our perception is lacking. With the usual eyes of the soul blinded, we need to adjust to the darkness before it yields its mystery to us. Hence the double virtue of patience and perseverance is needed in the initial stages to maintain the willed being of the prayer of loving regard over as long a period of time as is necessary. Like all transitional states, adjustment varies between individuals and depends in this case largely on the tenacity with which we cling to the remembrance of spiritual pleasures. To let them go, with thanksgiving for what they have given us, but without regret for their loss, is the necessary preliminary to any acceptance of the darkness, and with it, any expectation of further progress on the road to union with God.

Yet, once this initial surrender is made and we embrace the suffering and dereliction that entails, we do begin to discern that the pain is shot through with joy, that the darkness becomes less alien and that the void within and without is not empty of consolation. The Lord remains hidden, but he is present and, as in the Eucharist, the more we receive him with thanksgiving the more he gives himself to us secretly in the depths of our soul. The difference is that in the Eucharist, 'faith, our outward sense befriending, makes the inward vision clear', whereas in the prayer of loving regard, 'faith believes, nor questions how'. We have no 'outward sign' to acknowledge, only an intuitive sense that it is so. But that intuitive sense, which is faith operating in the dark, does open new avenues of perception which recognize that the hidden presence of God with us is not confined to those times spent in contemplation, but belongs to all times. We discover increasingly that St Paul's injunction that we pray without ceasing is becoming true for us because the Lord we love is present with us at every moment of our lives. We may overlay his presence with activity, be it of thought or feeling or practical works, but whenever we pause and let that activity subside, he is there, discovered secretly within us and around us, closer than breathing, nearer than heart-beating. God's hidden presence is not confined to times of prayer but possesses us through and through.

Of course, this has always been so, but until now we had not realized it, except perhaps intellectually. Now we know it to be so intuitively by faith alone, and this stirs up our hope that we shall yet see him as he is and girds our love with courage to surrender the whole of our lives unreservedly into his hands, because we are convinced that nothing will ever separate us from him and his love for us.

It is in this spirit that the loss of spiritual pleasures gradually becomes acceptable at all levels of our being, so that the pain subsides, the dereliction fades, and loss itself becomes recognized as a blessing and cherished as a sign of God's confidence in us. Spiritual pleasures become seen for what they are, good gifts lavished upon us by the Father's love to excite us and coax us into discipleship, to be enjoyed and used to attract us away from sin and unbelief towards faith and holiness. But such gifts will not carry us to union with God; only he himself can do this. Therefore God takes them away so that we may proceed further without them than would be possible with them. We shall find that there does remain an emptiness, a longing in the heart, but not because the pleasures that filled it before are gone, rather because God wishes to increase not only our faith but also our hope. Faith is to be changed into sight, but not yet, and hope will gain possession, but not now. Both, together with love, have further to journey before their fulfilment in the vision of God, a journey to which we shall turn in the next chapter.

But there remains the matter of the effect that the loss of spiritual pleasures has in other areas of the Christian life besides that of prayer. The sacramental life is to continue with the same regularity and commitment as before. The offering of the Eucharist and the receiving of Holy Communion remain central to our life, and the need for absolution in the sacrament of Reconciliation is undiminished. But, whereas in the past our feelings, our intellect, and sometimes even our body, received tangible benefits from the sacraments in the form of sensations of joy or peace or exhilaration, and so on, now these effects fall away and we are required to receive the sacraments as means of grace out of devotion to God alone, not for any side effects in our senses that we may receive. We are called to dissociate ourselves from such ideas and hopes, and come to the sacraments because God has ordained them for our good. We discover that the objective nature of the sacraments and the grace they convey to us mean more than any subjective spur to discipleship which they have given us in the past. Of course, sometimes there is a subjective experience still, but we should not expect or hope for this, nor cling to it if it comes. It is enough to receive and let God have his way with us.

Similarly with worship, its outward effects upon the soul usually disappear and we are left with the duty to join our fellow Christians in praising and glorifying God together, without the former sensual incentives. Indeed, now is the time for even greater attention to detail in worship, because while we are singing outwardly with our lips, our heart may be singing silent music within. We shall still be participating fully with the congregation, but now we are operating on two levels, and the temptation is to opt out of the common worship in favour of the individual. But temptation is the right word, because behind it lies the prompting of Satan to look upon ourselves as superior to the others in the congregation. But there are no such divisions within the body of Christ into first class and second class, because all are equally loved and accepted by Christ. Indeed, it is a humbling thought that there will be others present whose hidden life of faith in Christ has taken them further along the road than ourselves. We remain attentive to and actively participating in the worship of the Church, because without it we will drift off into an individual piety that loses the holy common touch and may even fall into error and schism.

Thirdly, the fight against sin and growing in virtue continues unabated. The fact that we have progressed sufficiently for God to remove spiritual pleasures, and the incentive that they have given to us to continue the struggle, does not mean that we have reached perfection. What it does indicate is that God now has sufficient confidence in us to trust us to maintain our momentum without repeating the pleasures that have flowed from former victories. In other words, the battle goes on, for love of God and his holiness alone, because we want to overcome the sin that is in us, and not because we get a 'spiritual high' out of the achievement. It also teaches us that the real victory is God's anyway and that it is his grace that enables us to triumph, not our enthusiasm for spiritual pleasures.

Exactly the same principle applies to the practice of virtue. We do not want virtue simply because it brings us pleasure — indeed then it would hardly warrant the name virtue — nor do we want virtue for virtue's sake, which is a purely moral control on our attitudes and conduct. Rather, we seek virtue for God's sake, so that we may serve him more effectively and efficiently. One of the delightful consequences of entering into the 'dark night' at this further level is that it frees us from all sorts of silly distractions and personal preferences, so that a genuine contemplative is usually level-headed, down-to-earth, sensible and practical. Not for him the anxieties of personal reputation or quibbles about taste and convenience; rather, for him, the practice of virtue is straightforward, yet sensitive to the needs of others, often disconcertingly honest, yet kind. Alongside the practice of virtue usually runs a sense of humour, though fortunately there is no such thing as a contemplative sense of humour. This profound blessing derives from the stripping away of our pretensions and the exposure of our foolishness in the 'dark night', so that the funny side of life impinges more immediately upon our humanity, and what the world sees as below its dignity the contemplative views as fair comment upon creatures who depend totally upon God for every breath they take and yet put on airs and graces which make them look ridiculously self-important. A contemplative can be a disconcerting person to have around because his sense of humour — be it gently ironic or rumbustiously hearty — is liable to highlight only too alarmingly so much of the nonsense that flows from our egoism.

In the following of Christ, the command of our Lord to take up the cross daily and follow him comes to life in the experience of the darkness and the stripping away of our power to direct our prayer into channels of our own choosing. The loss of self in order to gain our self comes home to us in the suffering of deprivation and loss that the darkness brings. But its application goes wider than prayer, for the cross becomes more firmly rooted in our hearts as the touchstone of faith, the standard of conduct, the source of grace and the promise of identification with our Lord. Our whole life is beginning to be marked interiorly with the marks of the nails and the wound of the spear. The acceptance of suffering in daily living becomes more and more an indispensable element in the call to discipleship. That suffering may be active, in the affliction that so often comes when we stand up for what is good and just and right and true. It may be that our vocation will include being crushed between political, economic or social forces. Whatever God calls us to do for him will bear the marks of sacrifice, and we embrace these out of love for him and because he calls us to love others for their own sakes, because he loves them also. Also, suffering will come passively when we experience within ourselves the ravages of illness or deprivation, and when we sit with another while he goes through an agony that we cannot relieve. There is no end to the variations of evil that will bring suffering to us, but the contemplative knows that the God who is with us is the God who suffers in us and dies for us, so that we may hold on to a dark hope even while we undergo the unendurable.

Lastly, there is the matter of 'life-style'. Here the issue is not so much what we have as how we regard it. The rich can be poor in spirit and the poor can be covetous and greedy. The key to 'life-style' is detachment, the ability to have but not to hold on to, to let go and not regret doing so, to be the steward but not the master of our possessions. Reference has already been made to food and drink and 'creature comforts' in the previous chapter. These remain necessary and good in themselves. The contemplative, being stripped of his spiritual possessions, is not fooled by the things he has around him. They are there to be shared generously and used appropriately, not turned into idols through covetousness nor despised as 'merely' material through an under-estimate of their actual contribution to the well-being of his life. We learn detachment from things most obviously when we lose a precious possession or break a treasured memento, and discover that it meant far more to us than we had imagined. Such small lessons keep us in good stead for the time when we may lose all our possessions, and for that moment which all must face, the surrender of all things, including our soul, into the hands of God at our death.

All these aspects of our life in Christ are enhanced thus when we enter into the transition from meditation and mental prayer into contemplation; and we should rejoice in the midst of our stripping that this is so, that God's generosity towards us has granted us this privilege of a closer following of the way of the cross.

But, there remains the matter of the content of meditation and mental prayer, and what has happened to them. At first sight, there appears to be total loss. Meditation is impossible. The parts of prayer have disappeared. We are assured that it was right to let them go, but perhaps we begin to wonder whether we could have salvaged something from them. At one level, the answer is that our meditations and our mental prayer are like the ingredients of a soup — once the cooking and blending and sieving of the ingredients is done, then no one ingredient can be recognized by itself any more, but all have made an essential contribution to the soup produced. Similarly, all the elements of meditation and mental prayer have been incorporated into contemplation. However, this view of the process does imply a rather rigid distinction in time between the contribution of meditation and mental prayer and the resulting practice of contemplation. In fact, this is not strictly so. Elements of mental prayer still occur and the need for some alternative to meditation remains.

Looking at the former more closely, we still fall into sin and need to repent, and while it is true that the sacrament of Reconciliation and the general confession at the Eucharist continue to bring us the assurance of God's forgiveness, nevertheless our sorrow for sin often demands an inclusion in our daily prayer as an integral part of the circumstances under which we pray. The distinction which is valuable here is the one between feeling sorry and being sorry for sin. It may be that, once the transition to contemplation begins, our ability to feel sorry dries up, and we are left with the pain of being sorry in the presence of God without being able to express our feelings. The contemplative may stand before the hidden presence with a heart that feels no sorrow but is profoundly sorry for its sins, so that that sorrow intensifies the agony it experiences as a further deprivation to be borne, accepted and embraced.

In a similar way, being thankful often becomes more important than thanksgiving supported by feelings of rejoicing or intellectual pleasure. Resting in the hidden presence of God in a state of thankfulness for creation and redemption replaces acts of thanksgiving that have fed and inspired mental prayer. The liturgical year, theological reading, the Scriptures and the accumulated intellectual material lodged in the memory, now resting quietly in the darkness, will provide a generalized context of thanksgiving to the practice of the prayer of loving regard, suffusing it with our awareness, not articulated but known, of the self-giving love of God towards us. In particular, this attitude of thankfulness, coupled with being sorry, replaces our former attention to the cross as a subject for mental prayer with a growing realization that the hidden presence in the 'dark night' is none other than the crucified one, who suffered for us on Calvary and remains united with his Father both in time and for all eternity.

Adoration, that natural development of thanksgiving from appreciation of what God has done for us into devotion to him for who he is in himself, remains as the core of contemplation, silently, gently, acknowledging that, despite our suffering and deprivation, the darkness is welcome to the soul as the state in which God is to be discovered anew, freed from the emotional and intellectual limitations of previous circumstances. Faith sustains adoration, independent of spiritual pleasures, and as the soul grows in devoted attachment to the hidden presence of God, so the loss of ecstatic states becomes not only acceptable but even welcome.

Intercession, on the other hand, appears to suffer a total eclipse. Lists of people and causes to be prayed for have become meaningless; any attempt to make petitions for particular needs is usually impossible; the general drive to intercession dries up. At the same time, we instinctively know that although intercession is not the heart of prayer, yet it is essential to prayer. Otherwise, there is nothing to prevent our spirituality becoming self-centred and indifferent to the world at large. Therefore, we must discover within the prayer of loving regard this element of concern for others. To do this, we should consider two potent scriptural images that relate petition and contemplation directly.

The first of these is the account of Aaron entering the holy of holies in the tent of meeting, wearing a breastplate, set with twelve precious stones, representing the twelve tribes of Israel. He appears before the hidden presence of God, symbolized by the ark of the covenant, bearing Israel on his heart. He stands before the ark as the throne of grace, presenting the needs of the people to God by the very fact that he is their representative and they are being carried in his heart into God's presence. He has no need to speak. Being in the hidden presence is his intercession. The second image is in the Letter to the Hebrews, where Christ is described as 'always living to make intercession for' us. The Greek verb, 'to make intercession', literally means standing in the presence of a superior on behalf of someone else, and it is the element of standing as a representative petitioner rather than the details of the petition which is upper-most in the meaning. So Christ is a greater Aaron who has entered the heavenly sanctuary to appear before his Father's throne, interceding for us, not by making spoken petitions, but by the fact that we are carried into the presence of God through being in his heart. So it is that we, as members of Christ, united with him by Baptism, are able to take part in his intercession by standing silently in the presence of the hidden God who sees what is in our heart and accepts our wordless concern as prayer for the needs of the world. So it is that the heart of the contemplative is most truly set at the heart of the world's sorrows, without being over-whelmed by petitionary prayer. Of course, sometimes intercessions are verbalized, usually outside times set aside for the prayer of loving regard. On these occasions, it is the pressing sorrow of the world's pain that leads us to seek to pierce the clouds of heaven with an arrow prayer, 'Lord, have mercy', 'Thy will be done', 'Lord, help them'. No need any more, to explain at length or to express our human anxiety. It is enough to cry out briefly in loving regard for our fellow human beings, believing and trusting that we shall be heard by the God whose hidden presence surrounds and sustains us and the rest of his creation.

Finally, there is the loss of meditation as a preliminary to mental prayer. Obviously, the move into contemplation, wrought passively in the soul by God, does not bring to an end the ability to think theologically. Otherwise, great contemplatives such as St Thomas Aquinas and St John of the Cross would not have written works of spirituality and theology of great academic distinction. Also, at a humbler level, the reading of the Scriptures and books of devotion and theology remain necessary, in order to keep the mind fresh and informed about Christian truth. There is no sense in which the prayer of loving regard induces in us either intellectual amnesia or worse, intellectual indifference. God still requires that we exercise our mental powers to the best of our ability. Anything less is a recipe for atrophy and bigotry. The difference is that whereas in the past, meditation as a formal exercise was helpful in stimulating mental prayer, indeed for many of us an indispensable preliminary, the practice of contemplative prayer now becomes the primary stimulus from which intellectual enlightenment emerges in our reading and thinking, done on other occasions. We do not seek meditation as the way into being in the hidden presence of God, but that hidden presence, dark as it is to the intellect, mysteriously inspires and illuminates the mind to work more intuitively, with more immediacy upon the exposition of faith and its consequences for the believer. The fruits of prolonged pondering by the mind, unforced, but peacefully active in its depths, often produces profound insights into the significance of faith and its application to life. Although such pondering often does produce intellectual pleasure, this is not always so, and it does not usually flow back into the prayer of loving regard, except for those whose psychological make-up is already highly integrated and settled around strongly linked emotional and intellectual faculties. For such people, of course, just as contemplation and mental prayer are never entirely exclusive, even so intellectual activity at an intuitive level and formal meditation still continue to operate in tandem, though the emphasis is likely to move steadily towards the former.

Even spiritual feelings do have their equivalent in the prayer of loving regard. We may have been stripped of them to lead us away from dependence upon the pleasure principle, but once the soul is settled in the practice of contemplation, there steals across it, not a sense of pleasure, but an awareness that all is well, that in the 'dark night' is the right place to be, and that the hidden presence of God will yield to us further insights for our benefit. A realization dawns that there is still far to go before union with God is attained but we are on the right road. It is to the detail of this potential development that we now direct our attention.

ELEVEN

The Three-fold Cord

When the convert begins to pray, he actively seeks to live by faith, hope and love, devoted to God. He pursues the way of the cross as the means of expressing his commitment, and progresses eventually to the point where he can go no further, and must be content to rest passively during a period of transition in which meditation and mental prayer are taken away and replaced by a more intuitive relationship with God. Led forwards into the darkness of contemplation, the disciple finds that the grace of God moves him onwards into a way of praying that is more simple, more silent, less self-centred, less concerned with pleasure. The strengths of the soul are no longer dependent upon stimulation to the extent that they were before and seek to find a new way to operate, suitable to the intense darkness they experience.

In particular, the abilities of the soul which we call the understanding, the memory and the will need to discover themselves anew within the 'dark night', and to discover how to direct the soul towards God within this different environment. The transition from meditation and mental prayer to contemplation is wholly God's work, and we rest passively in his hands. But once the transition is made, and we become accustomed to the new mode of prayer to which God has brought us, then we are called to build upon our experience and bring our understanding, our memory and our will into a closer alignment than before with the theological virtues of faith, hope and love. These three fundamental expressions of our relationship with God remain at the heart of the soul's progress to union, and, divorced from spiritual pleasures, will provide us with the sure way of growing into that oneness with God which is our desire. During this life, our union with God is to be a union of faith in the understanding, of hope in the memory and of love in the will. A further step towards the beatific vision is possible for a few with an extraordinary ability to suffer and to love over and above the capacity of most of us, and this will be touched on in the last chapter. But for the large majority of committed Christians this last step before the transfiguration of ourselves by the divine glory will be reserved for purgatory, and they live within the contemplative experience, seeking a union of faith, hope and love, that will require of them more than enough to test their commitment to the way of the cross.

In the case of our understanding, its power of discursive thought has run into the sand as a means of preparing us for prayer. Former intellectual pleasures that stimulated our meditation and mental prayer cease to be effective, and the understanding is darkened by the intense night it now experiences from God. Unable to benefit from these former delights, the understanding is required to remove its desire for satisfaction from what is now unobtainable and to attach that desire elsewhere. It is useless to pretend that the soul ceases to desire because it cannot have what it formerly enjoyed. To be so deluded is to invite shipwreck of the soul, in the form of desires, which should be directed properly, becoming unruly and debased. In the case of the understanding, the temptation is to fall prey to false intellectual ideas in an attempt to discover new pleasures to replace those taken away. The danger is that of always looking for something new, rather than clinging to what is true.

Of course, the attachment required of the understand-ing is that of faith in God, without the support of the intellectual delights that the understanding was formerly able to discover in theology. We continue to think theologically, but not to need the pleasures that such understanding used to bring. In prayer, the understanding believes in God and trusts God without being able to reason why this is so. The darkness of contemplation strips the understanding of all pretence in the presence of the incomprehensible and requires of it faith alone. What this means in practice is a daily surrender of intellectual constructs as damaging to prayer, and a willingness to let God have his way with us darkly and sovereignly. Whatever happens in prayer, we believe God is with us and his goodness will sustain us, even when we suffer deprivation, loss and dereliction. 'Into your hands I commit my spirit' is the word from the cross that commends itself to the new contemplative as his act of faith in the one who has stripped him of his old intellectual certainties, and now calls upon him to wait in the darkness unsupported. Faith is an obscure habit of the soul in which eventually the darkness within is accepted as necessary if faith is to be true to itself and true to God. Faith is the key to letting go old securities in order to find ourselves again in a new trusting relationship with God. It is rarely comfortable, either at first or even after years of experience. We may say on some days, 'I believe', but on others, 'I believe that I believe', or again, 'I want to believe', or again, 'I believe, please help my unbelief'. Clinging to God in faith, holding on to his incomprehensible and enigmatic presence in trust, believing without knowing quite why we believe, being buffeted and perplexed by the mystery of iniquity and the persistence of human suffering, yet accepting that faith in the goodness of God is the only way of living that is open to us if we are to find ourselves at the last, all these test us again and again, and require us to renew our attachment of faith in the understanding to the God who

is above all and in all and through all and was crucified
for our salvation on Calvary. Whereas before we were
able to think these things through and pray them
through in reasonable confidence of finding a solution,
now we rest in the darkness and find ourselves pierced
by them without any support or solution to hand. We
are crucified on the cross of circumstances and hang
there in unsupported faith.

And what is true for the understanding is also true for
our memory. In the past, the remembering of intellectual and sensual spiritual pleasures had renewed our
desire to pray. They were a stimulation which excited
our hope that they would be repeated. And sometimes,
perhaps often, they were. But all this is now past. The
memory can no longer recall former pleasures and hope
of their return fades. A dark aridity steals across the
soul, turning its refreshing springs into dry desert. The
deprivation is usually intense, and one can fear for one's
sanity. If the understanding is no more help, then at
least, if God were merciful, he would leave our good
memories behind! But it is not so. His mercy is obscure
to us as much as his goodness, and he calls us to move
on beyond hope in the return of spiritual pleasures to
hope in him alone as the source and goal of our delight.
What is past is over and done with. Only the future
remains bright with promise. And yet it is a future
whose brightness is hidden at the present in the 'dark
night' of hope. We are to detach ourselves from seeking
to recall past pleasures in the memory and to attach our
memory to God alone in hope. Daily, he asks of us to
hope for him, to extend our longing for him, to sigh for
him as our fulfilment and our joy. Unsupported by any
recalled delights, we are to delight in the Lord who is to
be our heaven and our possession in heaven, and to do
so without any expectation of release from the darkness.
As with faith, so with hope, there will be days when we
shall only hope to hope, or want to hope, or cry out in

the chasm of hope that seems like hopelessness or despair. The suffering and evil of the world will test our hope in God most cruelly and cause us to question in our hearts how much longer must Christ delay his coming. But we are to endure to the end in order to be saved, and to recognize with St Paul that no one hopes for what he sees, but only hopes for what is not yet his possession. We are crucified on the cross of circumstances because we hope in the providence of God and will not reach out for any other consolation.

But the purging of the understanding and the memory will bring us no benefit unless we also purge the will. In the past we have exercised our wills, choosing the good and rejecting the bad, partly because it is God's will for us to do so, and partly because of obedience and delight. We love God and we love spiritual pleasure. Now, we discover the latter is taken away from us by the 'dark night' and we are purged of spiritual pleasures in order to set our hearts on love for God alone. The maintenance of the will on the path of virtue becomes a matter of clinging in love to the God who plunges us into sorrow and grief. Our will is no longer supported either by an understanding that can stimulate intellectual spiritual joys nor by a memory that can recall former delights in the will. Instead, the will is expected to act in love, supported only by naked faith and hope. The right choices remain to be made, but the encouragement to do so is now entirely God-centred in love. Yet the love of God for us is as obscure as his goodness and mercy towards us, and as he calls us to move away from loving him for the sake of spiritual pleasures, so the love he now offers us contains little to attract us or stimulate us to love in return. Daily he asks us to love him, even though he causes us pain. He seeks a self-sacrifice of our will which imitates that of Christ's sacrifice on the Cross, without the prospect of any return by our former loves. As with faith and hope, there will be days when we can only trust that we love, or want to love, or cry out from the depths of dereliction that love is destroying us. The choices remain, and become more difficult, as sin and evil intertwine more closely and more confusingly with faith and goodness, so that they crucify us as our love for God becomes more obscure and yet more necessary to us. We are being nailed to the cross of circumstances by the love within us relying on his love for us and refusing to be satisfied with anything less as our ultimate good.

This triple purging of the understanding, memory and will by faith, hope and love, centred in God alone, is the destruction of intellectual pride and worldly wisdom and their replacement by a dark humility and foolishness. They contain within themselves a strength and a courage that will see us through this darkness to the vision of God. Faith, hope and love together unite the soul to God in the darkness of our minds and hearts, so that even though he slay us we will not forsake him. We have been tested in the furnace of affliction and have come through into a strange new state of existence, purged and refined of dependency upon pleasure and drawn into a dark, obscure, yet solid dependence directly upon God.

The state of contemplation is beyond comprehension by our intellect, because it is not grasped by discursive thought, open to repetition by forced acts of the memory, or capable of dissection by reason. Instead, it embraces our rational faculties, superseding them in two ways. First, it puts them to sleep, so that they rest content in the obscurity of the 'dark night'. And, secondly, they become aware that, although the soul is now settled in a way of prayer that is beyond them, nevertheless, they are strangely fulfilled, both because they have contributed towards the development of this new prayer through mental prayer and meditation,

and also because the practice of faith in the understanding, hope in the memory and love in the will provides
each with an obscure satisfaction that is not to be
confused with pleasure and yet brings an inner peace
such as the search for intellectual spiritual pleasures
cannot give. The peace of God which surpasses understanding steals silently and unexpectedly into the soul,
within the darkness of deprivation and suffering that the
onset of contemplation brings. Our intellectual faculties
are reconciled to God through faith, hope and love, so
that they find themselves united incomprehensibly with
his incomprehensible being. Deep speaks to deep, in the
wordless intimacy of attachment to God alone.

TWELVE

More than Ordinary

Up to this point, our development of the Christian life, and in particular, the practice of prayer, has been the result of our response to the grace of God working in the soul naturally. As such, we have only considered the ordinary experiences of our pilgrimage of faith, that are common to all who seek union with God. But the grace of God also acts supernaturally in the soul, bringing to us further experiences which God regards as individually necessary to us for our progress. To some, there may be many such experiences, to others, very few. Each is given what he needs, and in the way that is potentially beneficial.

However, we need to explore a little more fully the idea of supernatural influence before we go further. Despite the evidence of Scripture, including events in the life of Christ himself, and despite the witness of Christians in every generation, including our own, the concept of the supernatural is often rejected as superstitious or belonging to a former world-view which is no longer credible. This rejection derives from a modern view of the universe which is mechanistic and self-sufficient. God, if he is permitted to exist, does so on the fringes of creation and is deemed unable to 'interfere' with the autonomy of the human race. All phenomena, including our spiritual life, are explained as having a natural origin and, if the evidence is intransigent to scientific method, then it is consigned either to the in-tray of interesting problems yet to be solved or to the psychological 'catch-all' conveniently termed the unconscious.

Here they can be left until the right explanation turns up.

But, to do so not only does violence to actual experience, it also reduces God to being a dependent adjunct of a man-centred universe. It reverses the essential characteristics of the human and the divine, making God in the image of man, so that man becomes the sum of all things. When Christians, and especially professional theologians, try to take into their faith such a radical reversal of the roles of God and man, then they cannot maintain the supernatural, and even the concept of grace acting naturally becomes an embarrassment. They cease to speak of what in fact happens in the lives of Christians, so that they at best confuse and at worst drive doubts into those whose faith is weakened by their teaching.

Therefore, the restoration of the supernatural as an authentic and integral part of the relationship between God and man is a crucial contribution to an enclosed world, tied hand and foot to mechanical forces which we claim to harness in the name of progress, and then discover contribute little to our search for purpose or meaning as human beings, made in the image of God. Even the place of grace, operating naturally in our lives, is at risk as a phenomenon, irreconcilable to purely humanist considerations, unless the supernatural is affirmed. Grace is a seamless robe, no matter how it operates, and to deny one aspect of its working is to deny all. The Christian affirmation is that grace perfects our human nature, and the loss of any sense of grace in our lives is both a declaration that we are already perfected as we are and a despair of any personal improvement to our lives.

But to affirm that the grace of God acts in our lives for our good is to present only half the experience of the human race. There is also the shadow side of evil and sin. Just as the grace of God acts naturally to spur us on to faith and virtue, so the temptations of Satan press upon us naturally to draw us down towards unbelief and sin. At the natural level, the issue for mankind is that of choice, the exercise of the will. The grace of God needs to be appropriated and used to combat the temptations of Satan. Here is the inner struggle that lies at the heart of the reordering of our lives around the imitation of Christ and the following of the way of the cross. This we have discussed already in some detail.

However, in addition to this struggle at the natural level, there is a further struggle at the supernatural level. Just as our senses, our emotions and our intellect are influenced naturally by the divine and the demonic, producing a movement towards goodness or wickedness, so too, at the supernatural level, the divine and demonic influence the soul for better or worse by, on the one hand, giving it additional resources to lead the life of faith, and, on the other hand, tempting it by extraordinary promptings to sin and unbelief.

To make this clearer, let us look at three examples of supernatural influences at work in the life of Christ. First, at the level of the senses, when Christ takes Peter, James and John apart and he is transfigured before them, what the disciples see is a vision of divine glory shining from the humanity of Christ. Their physical sight actually receives a supernatural vision that appears as light. Their sense of sight is illuminated in an extraordinary way to show them that Peter's affirmation that Jesus is the Christ is true. Here we have the grace of God acting supernaturally through their sense of sight to confirm their new found faith. Secondly, at the level of the emotions, Jesus in the garden of Gethsemane struggles with the matter of the Father's will and an angel strengthens him in his agony. Here, the supernatural influence is to provide an extraordinary moment of emotional support at a time of extreme distress, enabling Jesus to face the cross and fulfil his purpose. Thirdly, at the level of the intellect, when Jesus is tempted in the desert, Satan leads him to the top of a high mountain and 'shows' him all the kingdoms of the world. Here there is no visible seeing but an experience of the supernatural — this time demonic — analogous to seeing, but taking place in the understanding, not through the eyes. This is a moment of extraordinary temptation which Jesus resists as being contrary to the Father's will. He rejects at once what is doubly tempting because it is the promise of both natural riches and supernatural power.

Happenings, such as these, have been part of most Christians' experience in one way or another. It was so for Mary at the annunciation, when she accepted her vocation to be the Mother of God. It is so at often crucial moments when God tests us and calls us on to further progress in the spiritual life, or when Satan sifts us to see whether we are wheat or chaff. The supernatural action of grace upon the senses, emotions and intellect tends to occur constructively during the early stages of our pilgrimage, to enhance and sustain our conversion — visions, voices, tastes and touches beyond the ordinary and unexpected transports of joy and hopefulness are commonplace. We are to recognize them as good gifts from God to deepen our faith, our hope and our love, and to encourage us to reformation of life. The test of whether such experiences are divine or demonic is the test of Jesus himself; by their fruits you shall know them. If what the experience produces in the soul is good, then it is of God; if it produces disquiet in the soul and the faltering of faith, hope or love, then it is to be rejected as from Satan. For, at this early stage, the senses, emotions and intellect are wide open equally to Satan's guiles and, therefore, we must take care not to embrace spiritual experiences of this kind naïvely.

Indeed, in order to be sure, it is best not to cling to any supernatural experience of any kind, good or bad, or try to recall it in detail, lest it contain a hidden snare that catches us unawares and traps us in Satan's clutches. The difference between God's grace and Satan's influence, acting supernaturally upon our senses, our emotions or our intellect, is that if God's grace acts thus it brings us a benefit which enriches the soul, whether we accept the detail of the happening or not, whereas Satan's influence for bad cannot touch us unless we choose to let him into our soul. Therefore, it is prudent to be indifferent to all supernatural experience as such, so that we do not rely upon it or desire to repeat it, and yet gain the benefit of it if it is from God.

This principle remains important when the intellectual faculties of understanding, memory and will are deprived of their natural way of working through the loss of spiritual pleasures, and are left empty and dark in contemplation. Although the natural working of grace is channelled into the pursuit of faith, hope and love in God alone, supernatural influences, both divine and demonic, continue to bear upon these intellectual faculties, producing the analogous experiences to the sensual ones already mentioned. Like Jesus in the desert, we are to reject the demonic immediately, so that Satan gains no entry into the soul, even though he disguise himself as an angel of light. But we are also to reject the detail of divine grace in the soul, lest we cling to it, instead of God. We receive its general benefit, be it an influence for virtue or the deepening of faith, hope or love, or the renewal of joy and hopefulness, and let go any particular insight, revelation or knowledge. Not only are particular details liable to lead us away from the life of faith and union with God, but the detailing itself may be disturbed, because our nature is not yet perfect and therefore not able to reflect God's grace without distortion. Many have gone astray by declaring, for example, hidden revelations such as the date for the end of the world or peculiar doctrines about the manner of Christ's presence in the blessed sacrament, instead of putting these notions on one side and simply receiving the general benefit of renewed hope in the coming of Christ or increased devotion to his presence in the sacrament. The general rule is to accept into the soul that which is good, general and obscure and to reject that which is bad, particular or clear, lest these latter replace faith, hope and love. The contemplative life is, of necessity, lived in the obscurity of the 'dark night' and any supernatural influence on the soul which is beneficial will not break that principle by attempting to put aside the need for faith, hope and love, those very things which are leading us to union with God. He remains our goal and our greatest good, above and beyond even his best gifts.

However, as and when the grace of God acts supernaturally in our soul to produce extraordinary experiences and we receive a generalized benefit, such as the impression on the soul of a word from God, e.g. have faith, hold fast, hope only in me, peace, be still, etc., or a general sense of heightened feeling of joy or hopefulness that is beyond pleasure, then these can be recalled with benefit whenever we need help in our contemplation and in the maintenance of our daily faithfulness to Christ. Such permanent impressions in the soul are there for our good, and we renew the grace they bring to us by recalling them regularly as moments when the grace of God touched us with a special blessing.

Often, the distinction between the divine and the demonic is a difficult one to make, that requires the guidance of a skilled director of souls. All who wish to pursue the spiritual life seriously should find such a person and confide in him or her entirely what happens to them. In this way, we can be advised clearly how to proceed. In addition, if the particular details are intended to bring a more general benefit to the Church at large, then these can be communicated and acted upon without the soul becoming attached to the contents. Most shrines and places of pilgrimage, for example, were founded through supernatural influence upon the souls of faithful individuals, of which two outstanding examples are the Lady Richeldis and the Holy House of Walsingham, and St Bernardette and Lourdes.

The key point about all supernatural influence upon the soul is that it always comes of its own initiative, with the soul being passive and receptive. When the influence is demonic, then it can and should be rejected by the will, but when it is divine grace it penetrates the soul and brings to the senses, the emotions and the intellect a spiritual blessing.

However, that blessing can lead to pain and deprivation as well as delight and satisfaction. For most of us, however, such experience would seem confusing and damaging to the life of faith because it appears to be demonic. Therefore it is experienced only by those of great physical strength and immense courage in the soul. For the majority, the life of faith is lived entirely within the prayer of loving regard, growing more and more dependent on God and united to him in faith, hope and love, and supported by recalled moments of positive supernatural blessings, darkly experienced and savoured.

But for some, this is not the end in this life. Our negative emotions, focusing on anxiety and fear, having lain dormant for so long under the goodness of the dark but supportive presence of God in contemplation, are now stirred up by supernatural grace to bring us to a new grief that plunges us beyond contemplation into an even deeper and more desolate darkness than we have hitherto experienced. The final purging has begun.

THIRTEEN

Without End

To pray is to be human and to be human is to pray. We have travelled far from the selfish prayer of the unawakened soul into the devoted prayer of the man of faith. The path has been characterized by growing closeness to God and conformity to his will. Contemplation has succeeded mental prayer and meditation, and the surrender of the pleasure principle has centred the understanding in faith, the memory in hope and the will in love for God alone. The influence of grace acting supernaturally has given the soul a hidden and obscure source of consolation in the midst of the 'dark night', to sustain it in the active work of contemplation. This is to be the way of prayer for most of us for the rest of our lives.

Depending on the psychological make-up of the individual, there will be fluctuations in the amount of silence and stillness practised in prayer but, in general, the movement is usually towards more simplification and resting in the dark presence of God in faith, hope and love. But for a few, a further step occurs which is analogous in the intellect to the dereliction experienced in the senses at the loss of spiritual pleasures, but far worse.

Just as the senses and the intellect come to the end of their usefulness in promoting spiritual pleasures, once they have moved the soul on from conversion into meditation and mental prayer and achieved considerable success in the reordering of the person upon the imitation of Christ, so now the supernatural operation of grace upon our negative feelings produces unexpected and extraordinary experiences of dread and fear, bringing the contemplative work of the intellect into darkness so that the soul finds itself plunged into grief, bereft of the dark presence of God. It seems that faith fails, hope disintegrates and love becomes too painful to bear. The three-fold cord that has united us to God in the understanding, memory and will snaps under the strain of supernaturally induced sorrow, as our feelings drive us into a loss of contemplation as we have known it. It is a terrible moment when it first begins to happen and is the onset of purging in the soul. Whereas up till this point, grace has supported our dependence upon faith, hope and love, now grace tears these from our faculties, asking us to rest in faith without faith, in hope without hope, and in love without love. We are helpless in the hands of God and he is piercing our heart with a series of horrors from which there seems no respite, no release except death.

The temptation is to despair of God and to doubt his goodness towards us. This is the last temptation of Satan, to make us deny that the God who afflicts us so terribly remains the good God who loves us and wants only our good. We are presented starkly with the ultimate affirmation of belief in the goodness of God, in the context of such horrible suffering that the soul recoils from its affliction. Often to make matters worse, our internal pain is misunderstood by those around us and their indifference, or even hostility, add to our burden. We are embattled within and without. Yet, under the hammer blows raining down on the soul, God is acting for our good.

The point is this, that up to this moment we have still been depending on our own intellectual powers, in that we have been refining our understanding, memory and will in the practice of faith, hope and love through the use of their natural strengths. They are detached from intellectual pleasures; now they must be further stripped. Also, we are not yet perfect and therefore not capable of receiving all the love that God wishes to give us. So, God brings the powers of our intellectual faculties finally to an end by the onset of a second period of transition in which we lie passive in his hands. This time he is detaching us not from the pleasure principle, but from dependence upon faith in the understanding, hope in the memory and love in the will, in order that we should be united with him directly in a darker love still. To do this, he purges us of our imperfections, enlarging our capacity to receive his love fully, and this tears at the very fibre of our being, rending us soul and body to be remade in his likeness.

The only way to survive this experience is to rest passively in the pain, affirming the goodness of God and his love for us, seeking not to escape his purging, and putting to one side any external affliction or persecution we may go through as nothing compared with the love of God which we wish to fill us. The soul rests, naked, derelict, bereft, unsupported, waiting for love to lead it where love wills.

This intense experience of suffering usually goes on for several months, even years, but there will be times of respite, lest we give up and fall away from God. Then the suffering returns in full force, driving us to surrender all our resources in the face of renewed affliction. This period of plunging grief alternating with return to the old way of contemplation is sometimes called spiritual betrothal, because the soul is being tested to see if it is worthy of union with the bridegroom. In the end, if the soul remains faithful to the last, spiritual betrothal gives way gradually to spiritual marriage, and the soul finds itself united directly with the divine lover. The purging is past and the soul rests quietly, trustingly, lovingly upon the bridegroom's breast, at one with him for ever, and at one with all creation, so that through his heart pours the world's thanksgiving and intercession directly to the heart of Christ.

Most of us are put through the suffering of crucifixion in one way or another, be it the loss of our faculties in old age, ill health, bereavement, loss of reputation or the ending of ambition, being treated unjustly or rejected unfairly. For many, the anguish these produce is more than they can bear and still maintain the same faithfulness to Christ that marked their previous commitment to him when their life was easier. Such afflictions cause many to fall away into bitterness or apathy. But, these crucifixions are as nothing compared with the purging that is spiritual betrothal, and those whom God brings to this particular share in the cross are necessarily few. They are those whose pilgrimage of faith has been marked by a generosity of spirit, a purity of heart and a singleness of eye beyond what most of us even begin to seek, let alone really desire. All things are possible to those who love God, but God alone knows if our souls are really capable of bearing the experience of purgatory on this side of the grave.

For those who are, spiritual betrothal is the plunging of the soul into union with Jesus in the garden of Gethsemane. Our wills live out in us the strain undergone by his will, our memory is reduced in us to the span of his memory and our understanding becomes to us what his was to him, as the dread and fear he knew sweeps over us also. He went on in this darkness to his betrayal and desertion by his friends, and so do we; he was cruelly treated, mocked and rejected, unjustly tried and condemned, and so are we; he was nailed to the cross and suffered both the internal agony of spiritual dereliction and the external pain of crucifixion, surrounded by the jeering crowds, and so shall we. Only Mary and John at the foot of the cross gave him their silent support, and only the intercession of the saints will be to hand to help us. But in the end, the last cry is to be, 'Father, into your hands I commend my spirit', the resigned surrender that is necessary that the purging may be complete and give way to spiritual marriage. The dead Christ on the cross and the darkened soul in purgatory both reach the final point of surrender from which comes the enigmatic but joyful resurrection to eternal life for Christ, and, for the soul, spiritual marriage in union with him for ever. Christ becomes our resurrection and our life, and one with him, we are filled with his joy and his peace.

Outside the walls of Toledo there is the small Romanesque church of Christo de la Vega, once dedicated to St Leocadia, whose tomb is there in the nave, before the high altar. Above the high altar is a nearly life-size crucifix. Christ is nailed at the feet and through the left hand, but the right hand reaches down towards the worshipper kneeling at the altar step. Anatomically, the pose is impossible, but the spiritual power of the invitation extended by Christ's right hand is overwhelming. He invites our petitions, but more than that, he invites us to join him on his cross, to share in his crucifixion, to participate with him in his work of salvation. Here in this crucifix is represented the meaning of prayer and therefore the final meaning of what it is to be human. Our prayer is to be the heart of a life dedicated to union with God and to bringing all creation to salvation in him.